Tear-Drenched Earth

Tear-Drenched Earth

Cinema and the Partition of India

John W. Hood

Orient BlackSwan

TEAR-DRENCHED EARTH: CINEMA AND THE PARTITION OF INDIA

ORIENT BLACKSWAN PRIVATE LIMITED

Registered Office
3-6-752 Himayatnagar, Hyderabad 500 029, Telangana, India
e-mail: centraloffice@orientblackswan.com

Other Offices
Bengaluru, Chennai, Guwahati, Hyderabad, Kolkata,
Mumbai, New Delhi, Noida, Patna

040883

First published by Orient Blackswan Private Limited 2024

ISBN 978-93-5442-469-4

Typeset in
Adobe Jenson Pro 12/13.75
by Le Studio Graphique, Gurgaon 122 007

Printed in India at
Balaji Books 600 0018

Published by
Orient Blackswan Private Limited
3-6-752 Himayatnagar, Hyderabad 500 029, Telangana, India
e-mail: info@orientblackswan.com

In memory of

Buddhadeb Dasgupta

... the desolate terrain
trembled with such great violence that the thought
soaks me once more in a terrified sweat.
The tear-drenched earth gave out a gust of wind,
erupting in a flash of bright vermilion,
that overwhelmed all conscious sentiment.

Dante, *Inferno: The Divine Comedy I,* Canto 3.
Trans. Robin Kirkpatrick (London: Penguin Classics, 2006).

Contents

Introduction

The Partition of India, which came as a condition of independence from foreign rule in 1947, was a cataclysmic assault on the country's socio-political integrity, the effects of which were suffered cruelly by millions of ordinary people. Indeed, the ramifications of the Partition are still being felt more than 70 years after the Radcliffe Line was imposed. Given the widespread hurt that was endured, the social upheaval that wantonly sundered the closest of relationships, the hatred that was inspired, and even the love that might have been discovered, the Partition was, ironically, a gold mine of stories for filmmakers. Perhaps it is somewhat surprising that it has not inspired more films than it already has.

The Partition had two manifestations, one in the west of the country and the other in the east, creating a new nation-state of two territorial wings: West Pakistan and East Pakistan, hundreds of kilometres apart. In the present work, there have been times when it has been of interest to make observations that are geo-culturally specific, but generally experiences such as communal hatred, rape, slaughter, social displacement, fracturing of families and loss of livelihood were much the same in the west as in the east, as they would have been anywhere else for that matter. It is worth noting that the Sikhs and their culture are infinitely more prominent in the region of the western Partition, and that the Bengali-speaking people of the eastern region formed a significant socio-cultural majority remarkable in itself. Beyond these actualities, what is represented on screen is of interest for *what* it is, rather than for *where* it happened.

The filmography on which this book is based is by no means exhaustive. I have made no attempt to work with a comprehensive list of all or even most of the films that are to any extent relevant; rather, I have selected those films that illustrate major points of interest arising out of the Partition experience. This is another way of saying that I have selected films which serve the chapter contents as I have devised them. The chapters are primarily thematic and only aspects of films that are pertinent to a particular theme are included in any particular chapter. For example, most of Richard Attenborough's mammoth *Gandhi* (1982) has nothing to do with the Partition, but Chapter 1 could not have been written without the consideration of those aspects of the film that are indeed relevant. In the opening chapter, I also discuss Ketan Mehta's *Sardar* (1993) and Gurinder Chadha's *Viceroy's House* (2017), films which offer some helpful historical information, such as insights on the growth of the movement for Pakistan and the arguments for the resistance to it. Of particular interest, I find, is the varied treatment of the major players—Gandhi, Nehru, Patel, Jinnah and Mountbatten—and the extent to which their personalities might have intruded into the filmmakers' interpretations of history.

The Partition was not well-planned. It was decided on and instituted in a hurry and so there were many consequences that betrayed its inferior conception, preparation and poor administration. Some of these were absurdly anomalous, even amusing, but most were of such seriousness that they could never be laughed away. Because of lines drawn on a map, new regulations and protocols, new prescriptions and proscriptions, and, indeed, new values and attitudes came into being. More seriously, there was the germination of new, often toxic, attitudes between people whose communities had lived in harmony with one another for centuries. Chapter 2 looks at a number of films dealing with quirks in the Partition narrative that indicate consequences far from the ideals of sound administration. Unforeseen opportunities emerged to be exploited, and by which to exploit, and large-scale inequity and injustice were the result.

One of the earliest films on the Partition, and certainly the earliest discussed in this book, is Nemai Ghosh's *Chinnamul* (1950). Chapter 3 discusses this classic film as a prelude to the broader examination of social dislocation in Chapter 4. *Chinnamul* deals with a number of pertinent issues arising out of the Partition, such as the lust for property on the part of some who goaded many of the Other community to leave, or the problems of accommodation and employment at the refugees' destination. However, dislocation can be seen as an all-embracing calamity, suffered to varying degrees by everyone who became an unwilling emigrant. Many of the outcomes of being uprooted, such as being separated from friends and family, becoming impoverished, or suffering physical and mental trauma are talked about at some length in Chapter 4.

Inherent in the Partition was the catalyst that fomented utterly base and irrational behaviour in otherwise decent people (and truly indecent ones as well). Serious hardship brought on by dispossession and displacement led to confusion, fear, despair and anger, an emotional tumult that sought culprits on whom revenge might righteously be executed. Laying blame in an emotionally charged atmosphere akin to mass hysteria was in fact an outlet for hatred—genuine, cultivated or conjured—which only generated further reprisals. Revenge was a mutual experience and, it seemed for a time, infinitely self-generating. Yet so much vengeance was emblematic and, therefore, unjust and irrational, as well as barbaric. If revenge had been taken on the actual perpetrators of a particular atrocity, the lynch law might have had an element of justice in it, given that punishment would have been administered to the culprits rather than to just anyone of the Other community. In fact, in most cases the perpetrators of savagery got away with it, so 'punishment' was administered vicariously in imposing reprisals, usually even more severe, on any individual or group identifying with the Other. So much of the violence and other iniquities depicted in the films discussed in Chapter 5 can be accounted for by the irrational lust for vengeance.

The demand for Partition arose mainly out of Jinnah's Two Nation Theory. Jinnah might have added a third 'nation', for Sikh religion and society are highly organised and there have been demands from time to time for a separate Sikh homeland. Sikhs played a central role in the turbulence associated with the western Partition of the country. However, whether or not Hinduism and Islam—or Sikhism too—can be regarded as nations is besides the point here. What is significant is that these three terms, denoting three religions, also have obvious communal applicability. There are many who are of no faith or who profess to be atheists, yet who identify as belonging to the Hindu, Muslim or Sikh community. So much of the Partition's strife had *communal* intent; *religious* interests were never a major or widespread issue. Nevertheless, when a struggle is daubed with religious nomenclature it can be perceived to take on the nature of a holy crusade. If the battle is being fought for God, there is all the more reason why the battle must be won and all the more glory in the sacrifice of life. In fact, men—and women—did some truly heinous things while invoking the name of God. Chapter 6 looks at films in which religion is seen to play a defining role in communal conflict.

The Partition brought about cataclysmic changes in the lives of countless people. Doubtless there were those in the mass migrations for whom the great displacement meant new opportunities and a relatively assured and successful future. These, however, were not typical—or at least their stories have not gained great currency. Perhaps many Muslims moving from India to Pakistan were able to make a better fist of things, and perhaps forced migration from India was less common than from what became the two wings of Pakistan. Fundamental to the definitive change in people's lives was the attack on cultural identity, which, in many cases, meant national identity. A number of films present those affected in one way or another by the Partition as left yearning for something that seemed irredeemable, and this loss was often vital to what many people understood as meaning in their lives. Chapter 7 discusses films in which characters must struggle to come to terms with a challenged identity or a new and alien identity necessitated by the pulling up of roots set deep or the inability to put down new ones.

Finally I thought it important to look at some post-Partition examples of the politics of division. In a democracy, radical differences in the social fabric are expressed through the ballot box and the parliamentary process. In its last years, undivided Pakistan had swung to the authoritarianism of military autocracy. India, however, continued to be the world's largest democracy throughout the years since Independence, with the exception of the 19-month-long aberration of the Emergency from 1975 to 1977. In 1971 came the culmination of years of dissension and disputation in the great sundering of Pakistan and the birth of Bangladesh, a parliamentary democracy at least for much of the time since its liberation. However, in India, in 1984 and 2002, communalism was deliberately exploited so that differences and sectarian assertiveness might be tested, not constitutionally but through communal riots and the accompanying killings and destruction. Chapter 8 has no overtly integral connection with the Partition, and might be regarded more as an afterthought on Partition issues. Nevertheless, it aims to be an afterthought with a warning: that a strong and successful state cherishes the politics of cohesion, and that the politics of division can only be destructive—one of the fundamental lessons of the Partition of 1947.

This book is not intended as a text for 'film studies', though one would surely hope that students of cinema, whatever the nomenclature and proclivities of their courses, will find it interesting. Still less can it be described as 'history', even though it deals with a major experience in the history of the Indian subcontinent and refers to a number of characters whose place is comfortably entrenched in works rightly regarded as 'histories'. This book, rather, is an endeavour to appreciate certain salient features of the 1947 Partition of India, the bitter pill that accompanied the joyous cup of Independence, as represented in films, most of them worthy to at least some degree. However, apart from comments more incidental than germane, there has been little deliberate intention to offer film criticism as such, for the context *is* the substance—the Partition, especially its essentially human aspects, as represented in cinema. Because films usually deal with fiction, much of the discussion in these pages moves in generalities, while even specific characters often represent a human quantum far greater than any particular individual. Of course, there are films that present actual historical characters, and in Chapter 1, for example, I found it interesting to show how different directors offer quite divergent treatments of certain prominent leaders.

I have not considered it meaningful to distinguish, in this book, between commercial cinema and independent cinema. The focus is on the treatment in cinema of a calamity unprecedented in scale and devastation; the genre of cinema is, usually, immaterial. However, in Deepa Mehta's *Midnight's Children* (2012), which is not discussed in this book, there is an appealing allusion to popular cinema in the context of the birth and development of two new nation-states and, in particular, the Partition that brought them into being. Germane to the narrative of *Midnight's Children* is a classic narrative ingredient of Hindi cinema, which is the story that evolves out of babies being swapped at birth. 'Being swapped' might be a euphemism or an extreme understatement for the indiscriminate and extensive sundering of families, friendships and other relationships that occurred along with the birth of the two new nations. Millions of people lost their loved ones—some temporarily, many permanently—and identities and birth rights were blown away on the winds of violent change. If the entire Partition nightmare could be condensed into a single film, it would seem far too incredible even for Bollywood.

one

The Ominous Burden of Power

Prior to 1940, the notion of partitioning India along communal lines had been given some tentative and vague consideration; it was largely kite-flying and little more than scratching the surface. It was not until the Lahore Resolution of March 1940 of the Working Committee of the All-India Muslim League that partition became the fundamental plank for the League. A mere seven years and four months later, the details of the Punjab Boundary Award were announced and India was partitioned to allow for Pakistan, a new nation for Muslims, to be carved out of it. It would be an understatement to say that the process was one in which careful detail was sacrificed to the dubious benefits of haste. Virtually instantaneously, India was plunged into nightmarish uncertainty, one that had been simmering for months already. With a long nightmare of horrible killings, rape and abductions, an orgy of wanton destruction and theft of property, it was a time that flourished on the widespread ignorance of millions, who had neither been consulted nor adequately informed about the Partition. The politics of bigotry was flaunted without restraint, while the once proud imperial administration fled the country in a most impolitic dispatch.

It must have been relatively easy for the British to order the drawing of two fateful lines on the map and then go home to join in the collective licking of war wounds and embark on a life without India. However, those lines on the map caused millions of innocent people to suffer devastating dislocation, separation from loved ones, wholesale loss of property and means of livelihood, and slaughter, rape and other forms of brutality. The lives of up to two million people were sacrificed to the lines on the map, while some 14 million were displaced from their homes. In addition, there was the tremendous cost of the destruction and damage to property and crops, as well as the great loss of livestock. The immediate and short-term effects of the Partition were infernal and its corrosive ramifications are still being played out, more than 70 years later.

There are some people—mostly, one might presume, living in Pakistan—who hold the Partition to have been necessary and worthwhile. There are many more throughout the subcontinent who think of the truncation of India as a catastrophe, one that could have been avoided. To adhere to this latter view is to imply culpability, for the Partition of India did not just happen, but was, indeed, caused to happen. There were those who bore the burden of power and on whose shoulders the blame must rest. Most commonly, Jinnah is singled out for condemnation due to his intransigent insistence on a separate state for Muslims. His Majesty's Government and the last three viceroys might also be blamed for going beyond neutrality in their deliberate cultivation of relations with Jinnah and the Muslim League, seeing in the creation of Pakistan the potential for continued British influence in South Asia and the Middle East. There is also an argument, though a weak one, that condemns the leaders of the Indian National Congress, specifically Nehru and Patel—and even Gandhi—for a perceived weakness in caving in to a compromise with Jinnah.

As the country at last took its final steps towards independence from foreign rule, the underlying tension between unity and division made the burden of power indeed an awful one. Three films which give substantial emphasis to the political evolution of the Partition are discussed in this chapter: Richard Attenborough's *Gandhi* (1982), Ketan Mehta's *Sardar* (1993) and Gurinder Chadha's *Viceroy's House* (2017).[1]

Attenborough's *Gandhi*

Attenborough's film is something of an epic, running for a little over three hours. Nevertheless, much has been left out, such as, the often controversial relationship between Gandhi and Tagore; the telling disputation between Gandhi and Subhas Chandra Bose, which is merely alluded to; the remarkable peace-making venture in Noakhali, which is briefly reported; and the last premier of Bengal, Huseyn Shaheed Suhrawardy, seeming to come in out of the blue and remaining, though saying nothing, until the end of Gandhi's fast in Calcutta. Indeed, the specific politics of both the eastern and the western region, which would accommodate the birth of Pakistan, are neither considered nor examined. Clearly the writer, John Briley, and the director recognised the need for precision and conciseness, a feature that affords both screen economy and relative simplicity.

While the avoidance of depth and complexity might make for more readily comprehensible cinema, it would also disappoint those who would like to see the major questions at least raised, if not addressed. The most basic of these seeks to know why Jinnah was so insistent on dividing the country. In an exchange with Gandhi, Nehru and Patel during a break in the discussions with the viceroy, Jinnah says simply, 'I will not stand by and see the mastery of the British replaced by the mastery of the Hindus.' The Muslims in British India were a sizable minority, and prior to the advent of British rule, the Muslim emperors of the Mughal Dynasty had ruled large parts of the country. Community relations between Hindus and Muslims were generally peaceful, with countless instances of one community sharing in the celebration of the other's festivals, for example. That an independent India with a Hindu majority would be bad for its Muslim minority is a claim that Attenborough's Jinnah is not called upon to substantiate, nor is his Mountbatten obliged to defend the blatant divide-and-rule policies of the British from the late nineteenth century right up to the Partition.

As a clear illustration of the extent to which Gandhi was willing to go in order to prevent what he called 'the vivisection of India', Attenborough recreates a scene in which Gandhi tells Jinnah that he wants Nehru to renounce his claim to be the prime minister in favour of Jinnah, giving him the option to appoint whoever he wants as his ministers—all Muslim, if need be. Of course, the suggestion is nothing more than an expression of earnestness and goodwill, naively ignoring the certainty of the horrible reaction of the majority if they were to be ruled by the minority. Nehru states his willingness to go along with his Bapu's wish, but makes it clear that 'out there, there is rioting because Hindus fear you are giving away too much.' Patel adds, 'If you did this, no one would control it. No one.' There is a long pause and then the camera focuses on Jinnah, who offers the minatory warning: 'It is your choice. Do you want an independent India and an independent Pakistan, or do you want civil war?' Here is the man who was largely responsible for the dreadful carnage of Direct Action Day in the August of the previous year—something which is glossed over in this film—holding his trump card, the threat of more dreadful carnage. However, this is somewhat ambiguous: would he be responsible for the civil war, or would the disaffected Hindu majority? In Attenborough's film, there is no bringing Jinnah to account, except by the right-wing extremists of the Rashtriya Swayamsevak Sangh (RSS),[2] who are seen a little later shouting 'Death to Jinnah!', with Gandhi's future murderer, Nathuram Godse among them and the sinister Vishnu Karkare lurking in the background, and it is Gandhi who confronts and chastises them.

Naturally, Attenborough seeks to lionise Gandhi, and that is not necessarily inappropriate. He is beyond question one of the great forces of modern history and one of the most inspiring moral giants of all time. The record, indeed, is replete with his political mistakes and errors of judgement—which pedantic critics hasten to magnify—but it is his moral stature that will always have appeal and that is what Attenborough exploits. Even at the end of the film, when Calcutta is emerging from its days of insane blood-letting and destruction, there is a moment of exceptional moral strength, given poignant force by the performance of Om Puri as a man terrified of his own conscience.

Attenborough allows his Jinnah to escape being seen as a culprit with his equivocal presentation. From his first appearance in the film, he is consistently sour, humourless and sullen. His courtesy is formal though not unfriendly, and his apparent discomfort with Gandhi and his ideas might suggest a pronounced dislike but his attitude never breaks into open hostility. His last line, offering the choice of either independence with partition or civil war, might be interpreted by his critics as the threat of a bully or by his apologists as a sad recognition of a grim reality. And so, Jinnah leaves the film, except for an implied presence in a brief scene depicting the flag-raising ceremony during the celebration of independence in Pakistan (presented as following the Indian ceremony but held, in fact, the day before.[3])

In accordance with the intention to keep the focus on his hero, Attenborough avoids historical controversy, leaving the question of blame for the Partition to others, or rather, not acknowledging it at all. The last viceroy, ultimately responsible for the transfer of power, comes out of the film utterly blameless simply by being innocuous. He is presented as a cardboard cut-out, seemingly out of the pages of *The Boy's Own Annual*—handsome, charming and urbane, and a formidable hero, if the mass of medals on his brilliant white uniform means anything. He is one of the least significant characters in the film in terms of the narrative dynamics.

In *Gandhi*, the inclusion of the Partition itself, while essential to the historical narrative, is primarily done to reveal the film's hero in the depths of disappointment and also to show him as a special kind of hero, albeit one without medals or even a uniform to pin them to. As the joys of independence melded into the shrieks and cries arising out of the enormity of the Partition, Gandhi was approaching the age of 78, when men as a rule no longer put themselves in dangerous and violent situations, or calmly face both adulation and threatening abuse, nor deprive their bodies of food for days on end. Attenborough shows us the Gandhi who stood up to the notion of partition, seized the menace by the throat and shared those perils with millions of his ordinary countrymen. The film ends as it had begun, with the assassination by a twisted fanatic—and the vast funeral procession—of one regarded by millions as a saint.

Sardar

Sardar also focuses on one man, Vallabhbhai Patel, but this film is much more of a straightforward political biography than a hagiography. After about 20 minutes of pre-titles introduction dealing mainly with Patel's summary conversion to Gandhism and his successful leadership of the Bardoli *satyagraha*, the film jumps straight to the Simla Conference of 1945 and into the thick of the ensuing partition controversy, offering up about two and a half hours to the political history prior to India's freedom and division, and some three years beyond. Ketan Mehta's historical focus is, therefore, more concentrated and more extensive than Attenborough's.

While Patel is, naturally, the focal character throughout the film, for much of this cinematic account of the controversy that dominated the last two years of the British Raj, the character of Jinnah is prominent, not in screen time but in the force that he commands over the narrative. Mehta's Jinnah is uglier than Attenborough's, lacking somewhat in urbanity and polish, noticeably brusque and disobliging. He conveys, and is buoyed by, a dogged intransigence and a wilful negativity, and so readily evolves as the villain of the piece. Given that he holds the terrible trump card—the threat of direful violence—he is a villain to be taken seriously.

As the proposals of the Cabinet Mission create headaches and arouse intense feelings, Jinnah's veneer of dignity wears thin and he threatens *jihad* if Pakistan does not become a reality. A taste of that dreadful violence is then given on 16 August 1946, and the days following, in what is known as the Great Calcutta Killings or what Jinnah euphemistically called 'Direct Action'. Mehta gives us black-and-white file footage of mobs surging through the streets of Calcutta; newspaper headlines speaking of 'unprecedented violence', giving the death toll as it climbs from 90 to more than 1,000; file shots depicting vehicles on fire, dead bodies strewn in lanes and horrible shots of widespread destruction. Jinnah ought to have borne responsibility for this horrible carnage, but he does not seem to have even been censured.

Mehta's handling of the polemical material is always informative though sometimes blandly didactic. After a vibrant sequence showing some of the leaders arriving at the viceroy's residence in Simla, including Nehru on horseback, there is a sequence depicting the proceedings around the conference table. Even when speaking in an Anglo-inflected Hindi, Wavell is appropriately pompous, but the other leaders are notably wooden—simply stating their positions—with Maulana Azad affirming the Congress' view that India should stand united, and Jinnah emphasising that nothing can proceed without an acknowledgement of Pakistan. This prompts Baldev Singh to raise the notion of a separate Sikh homeland, while Dr Ambedkar reminds the meeting that the country's 60 million untouchables also represent a communal distinction. In his insistence that the Muslim League alone should have the right to nominate Muslims to any office, Jinnah reveals a touch of what will soon be seen as his characteristic waspishness, but apart from this there is no real drama or character interaction. What is achieved is a clear display of divisiveness and stubbornness.

The suspicion that the British government favoured the Muslim League in the partition controversy is hinted at in a scene depicting a meeting of Congress leaders in which Nehru refers to the Quit India Movement in 1942 when hundreds of Congress leaders and important members were summarily locked away, effectively silencing the major force behind the movement for Indian independence and giving Jinnah free rein in cosying up to the British, especially after Wavell's appointment as the viceroy in September of the following year. The closeness between the League and the government is underlined again in a scene in which Wavell tells Sir Stafford Cripps that their aim should be to make the Congress feel as though India remains united, and also that Jinnah gets his Pakistan. The compromise that would materialise from the Cabinet Mission's Plan B would be the splitting of the Hindu and Muslim populations of Punjab and Bengal, thus creating a truncated Pakistan which would be unacceptable to Jinnah. Eventually, however, he would have to accept those divisions.

The discussions—or reiterations of obstinacy—continue in an endeavour to formulate a scheme acceptable to both sides. Jinnah is positive about one proposal, Gandhi rejects it as 'reeking of Pakistan'. Maulana Azad comes up with a compromise which Jinnah immediately rejects, even demanding that the Muslim League should form the Interim Government. He then petulantly declares an all-or-nothing stance.

Jinnah is now shown to be menacing. He threatens that an all-out jihad will be the consequence of not getting Pakistan, and as though as a forerunner to it, we see the file footage pertaining to Calcutta following Jinnah's declaration of Direct Action on 16 August 1946. Sadly, the violence was not restricted to Calcutta or to just a few days in the middle of August. There is mention of riots spreading all over the country, especially in Rawalpindi, Karachi and Bombay, and flaring up intermittently in many other places in the period before, during and after the Partition. Wavell, it is said, would do nothing about the violence during his term of office as he judged it to be a states' issue; maybe he was loath to stay the hand of Jinnah. By the time the last viceroy took office, there seemed little that actually could have been done.

Patel is depicted as having a tactical understanding of Jinnah, and some dramatic interest is lent to the film with his endeavour to react appropriately in the light of that understanding. However, the nearness of a *fait accompli* is clearly suggested in the acknowledgement that the demands of the Muslim League will not stop until Jinnah gets what he wants. Nevertheless, Patel declares that Jinnah must state in writing that Direct Action will be withdrawn and that the Muslim League's participation in the Interim Government will be unconditional. Moreover, he stresses that the League must not be given the Home Ministry—which Wavell is thought to have wanted—as that would give them Pakistan on a plate.

A newspaper headlines sequence tells us that the League joins the Interim Government, accepting the Finance Ministry. Patel suspects the deliberate refusal of the League to cooperate in government, and another headlines sequence refers to the friction in the Interim Government. Once more the Muslim League stamps its foot and violence flares up, and there is now a short but disturbing scene in which Patel is seen being driven through a riot-torn area with houses ablaze, people in panic and slaughterers at work.

Mehta has his eponymous hero observe that the Congress is being dragged along by the viceroy on one side and Jinnah on the other. Clearly, Patel sees Wavell as a kind of silent partner to Jinnah, with the Congress lurching towards an unavoidable acknowledgement of Pakistan. His secretary, V. P. Menon, advises that the plan for a united India can be successful only if Jinnah relinquishes his demand for two nations, but civil war would erupt before he would do that. Menon sees the writing on the wall and so, one feels, does the pragmatic Patel. Menon argues that if a partition should occur while the British are still in India, then East Punjab and West Bengal could be saved and power might be transferred peacefully. What Menon foresees would indeed eventuate, though peace would not. Ultimately, both Nehru and Patel see no option but to accept Menon's advice.

Wavell is replaced by Mountbatten, and Jinnah must ensure that the new viceroy does not throw up any obstacles. He continues to prevaricate, saying no to everything, until he gets every inch of territory possible. A date is set for the award of independence to a partitioned India, and Maulana Azad seeks to offer solace to Abdul Ghaffar Khan with the profoundly ironic words, 'Brother, these are but lines on paper. They cannot separate our hearts. And I am sure that with time these lines will disappear.' More than 70 years have passed and the inseparable hearts have stopped beating, but the lines are still there, although the Bangladesh War of Liberation of 1971 rendered a seismic change in their significance.

There is file footage of the first Independence Day. We see the capital adorned with festive lights, there is a shot of Nehru addressing the Assembly, there are newspaper headlines proclaiming India's freedom, a gun salute, the new flag and a teeming crowd outside the Red Fort. It is all slightly dampened by Gandhi's words: 'Tonight we'll be celebrating with tears in our eyes.'

Attenborough, his focus firmly on his hero, gives us a Partition in passing, an event that would seem to have happened as part of the natural course of things. His Mountbatten is more of a decoration than an integral functionary, and while his Jinnah is querulous and obdurate, his urbanity shields him from being seen as sinister, and still less, in any way culpable. Mehta's Mountbatten is also a good-natured bauble, but his Jinnah is churlish and unlikeable, a pig-headed menace. In *Viceroy's House*, the notion of responsibility for the Partition is more subtle, complex and shadowy.

Viceroy's House

The most salient difference between *Viceroy's House* on the one hand, and *Gandhi* and *Sardar* on the other is the fictional narrative that runs parallel to, and is at times interwoven with, the interpretation of the historical material. It is, unsurprisingly, a love story, one inflected by Bollywood in that the partnership is made awkward by the presence of a second suitor; the affair evolves into a catastrophe but, by a stroke of fortuitous desperation, is ultimately redeemed from tragedy. It is worth examining this fictional narrative carefully in the context of the larger historical narrative to show a relevance, whereby it may be seen as a microcosmic representation of a number of elements being played out on a monumental scale.

Jeet Kumar and Aalia are notable employees of the Viceroy's House—he, as an under-valet, close to the Viceroy himself, and she, in a public relations role, close to the Viceroy's daughter, Lady Pamela. They meet soon after Jeet begins his employment there, some years after they knew each other in the Punjab; Jeet had been a junior penal officer and had come into contact with Aalia's father, Ali Rahim, when he was imprisoned for 'marching with Gandhiji'. Aalia and her mother were not permitted to visit Ali Rahim in jail, but after he lost his sight there, Jeet forged a relationship with him, reading to him and helping him to do the things a sightless man could not do. Apparently it was this care for her father that formed the basis of Aalia's fondness for Jeet and it is Ali Rahim's enduring debt to the boy that encourages her to maintain affection for him.

Aalia's father was a Gandhian nationalist who had courted imprisonment. Jeet never knew his own father, as he was killed in the Jallianwala Bagh massacre in 1919. Both Aalia and Jeet carry patriotic baggage while curiously employed at the epicentre of colonial power, and both are educated and have creative hopes for their role in the imminent new India. He is a Hindu and she is a Muslim. To make matters less simple, a complication was unwittingly created by Aalia's mother who, just before she died, expressed a wish for her daughter to marry Asif, who is soon to return to India from England where he has been serving in the British army.

Like so many of the others employed in the vice-regal residence (and they seem indeed to be legion), Aalia and Jeet are dismayed at the announcement that the country will be partitioned under what is already being called 'the Mountbatten Plan'. Both leave the Viceroy's House, she peacefully, and he, most improbably, after assaulting Mountbatten himself and threatening him with a knife. Their story will be revisited in a later chapter.

The antagonism and violence between Hindus and Sikhs on the one hand and Muslims on the other is shown to be a fact of India that nothing can change. However, there is no endeavour to even suggest that the acrimony and consequent brutality might have been orchestrated. Jeet tells Mountbatten that in his childhood in the Punjab, Hindu, Sikh and Muslim children played together, with the Muslims celebrating Diwali, and the Hindus and Sikhs celebrating Eid together. The transcending of the communal divide by, first, Jeet and Ali Rahim, and then Jeet and Aalia, is focal to the narrative and clearly suggestive of the view that communal hostility is not innate to Indian society but, as the film's Nehru tells Mountbatten, a consequence of the divide-and-rule policies of British colonialism.

The opening section of *Viceroy's House* establishes the fictional narrative by dealing with Jeet's recruitment to the vast staff of the vice-regal palace against the background of the domestic preparations being made for the imminent arrival of the new Viceroy, his wife and their daughter. It is not simply a matter of sweeping the carpets and dusting the chandeliers. Indeed, we see a veritable army of liveried lackeys, not one with a shirt untucked or a turban even slightly askew, sweeping, dusting, cleaning and rearranging the interiors of this immense and grandiose establishment built to house the second-most important person of the British Empire. One might accept that such conditions are appropriate to the position, but while one may not feel qualified to question the necessity for features such as 34 reception rooms, 34 state rooms, 10 private dining rooms and a cinema, all of which 'make Buckingham Palace look like a bungalow', one may readily marvel at the notion of the cost of running such an establishment, a cost met by the people of a country notable for its pervasive poverty. A telling adjunct to this is a little scene in which two liveried servants bring in a silver salver bearing the food for the Mountbattens' pet dog. The cloche is raised to elicit a gasp from Lady Mountbatten who has 'not seen chicken like this since before rationing'. A little later a large group photograph reveals the three Mountbattens with their household staff of more than 130 members.

The matter of the transfer of power is specifically introduced through a meeting of the provincial governors. There is a general feeling of pessimism concerning the alleged lack of integrity of Indians, the conditions prevailing ('In Bengal the violence is compounded by a famine'[4]), and the communal antagonism throughout so much of the country. Mountbatten's Chief of Staff, Lord Ismay (known to his peers as 'Pug') seeks to assure them that the man for the hour has come. On this basis, we might reasonably expect that after this Mountbatten will be lionised somewhat and be shown to be a man of action who intelligently disentangles the communal conflict that has been allowed to develop too far. That expectation will be disappointed. Gurinder Chadha's Mountbatten will be shown to be as ineffectual as his counterparts in both *Gandhi* and *Sardar*.

In a moment of despondency, Mountbatten tells his wife of his grave concern at the continuing violence which, he says, the British do not have the means or the manpower to contain. He also mentions Ismay's view that Pakistan is inevitable. It would seem that the simplest way of enabling the return of peace would be to give in to Jinnah's demands; India would be divided, but at least the violence would stop. The naiveté of this view is not yet evident, and Lady Edwina advises him to talk to Nehru first. Nehru is categorical that a divided India would be unacceptable and that it is ironic that the last Viceroy would be seeking a solution to the problem that British divide-and-rule policies have created. Mountbatten agrees that a division of India would be a tragedy, prompting Nehru to plead with him to convince Jinnah of that.

Mountbatten meets Jinnah at the Viceroy's House. The camera takes in the sumptuousness of the place, in which Jinnah seems to be very much at home, remarking initially on his time at Cambridge in an attempt to establish a rapport with the Englishman. He proceeds to argue that Muslims are a minority of about a quarter of the population and would likely be repressed in an undivided India. He then goes on to declare that the Hindus and Sikhs residing in Pakistan would be given every freedom to which the Muslims were entitled. He does not say what would make the minority in Pakistan better off than the one in India. What is indeed clear is his resolve, backed up by a somewhat alarming expression of personal invective towards Gandhi and Nehru, something that is not as evident in the other two films.

The hope for a peaceful, united India is shown to be fading in a mixture of genuine and mock-up file footage—some of which is quite confrontational—of riots in the Punjab and their consequent devastation. This is, of course, to Jinnah's advantage, for as long as such troubles continue, his Pakistan solution seems to make more sense. Ismay points out to Mountbatten the powerlessness of the British to stop or even contain the violence, given the acute shortage of manpower left by the early departure of so many British troops, and it was unthinkable that Indian troops would fire on Indian citizens. There is a cut to a shot of Gandhi spinning, then another cut to Gandhi and the Congress leaders in discussion with Mountbatten and Ismay. Nehru and Mountbatten seem to agree that a partition would be acceptable as a harbinger of peace, and that a division of Punjab and Bengal was the best available option. As Gandhi still tries to argue for unity, communal tensions run high in the army of servants outside the door and violence erupts. Although this is probably quite unrealistic, it is nevertheless an effective metaphor for what is happening in the country at large.

There is news of more violence, corroborated by archival material. A little mock-up file footage shows the viceroy in London for meetings with Atlee and Churchill, and then he returns to India having had the government accept what was now being called the Mountbatten Plan for the transfer of power, also involving the partition of the country. There is a meeting with leaders in which Jinnah complains of not getting enough, describing the award of Pakistan to be a 'moth-eaten' one. His obduracy continues for a little longer until Mountbatten makes it clear that it is divided Punjab and Bengal or nothing. It is at this point that a key figure in the whole affair, not seen in either *Gandhi* or *Sardar*, is introduced: enter Sir Cyril Radcliffe.

The question regarding *who* made the decision to appoint Radcliffe to the task of dividing India within the space of five weeks is probably irrelevant, though we might well ask *why* a man who had never set foot in India before and who knew next to nothing about the country and its people was appointed to this most daunting task. There must have been dozens of experienced and knowledgeable civil servants in India eminently better qualified for the job. Nevertheless, Radcliffe, at least in this film, does suffer qualms of conscience concerning the grim enormity of the job and his personal inadequacy for it. We see him expressing his concerns to Ismay, who then shows him a policy document drawn up by Churchill two years before, setting out the future of India. Attached to the document is a map of a partitioned India, drawn up by Lord Wavell the year before that. Ismay tells Radcliffe that it comes from the highest authority, and that even Mountbatten knows nothing of it.

The papers that Ismay shows Radcliffe shed a different light on the question of responsibility, or blame, for the Partition of

India. A title card before the opening titles tells us that the film draws ideas from two books, one of which is *The Shadow of the Great Game* by Narendra Singh Sarila.[5] This exceptionally well-researched work fastidiously documents the argument that the foremost of British concerns in the likelihood of their leaving India was the protection of their oil interests in the Middle East in the event of any Soviet Russian push southward. A Britain-friendly Pakistan, as distinct from a non-aligned India, would give Britain a base in the region that would serve its advantage both in the Middle East and in Southeast Asia. It might seem apparent now that the British warmth to Jinnah and the Muslim League during the 1940s might well have been a matter of nurturing British interests after the transfer of power. Sarila includes in his book the maps drawn by both Wavell and Radcliffe; the two are very similar in their concept of West Pakistan, but differ significantly on the proposed eastern wing.

While the Radcliffe of *Viceroy's House* fears that the award will lead to carnage, Mountbatten clings to the belief in a partition's potential to reduce the violence—a belief that, as soon became evident, was horrendously misplaced. Radcliffe, a man of principle and conscience, refuses to accept payment for the work he has done, and goes on to show Mountbatten the document that Ismay had made available to him. It would seem unthinkable that Ismay and Radcliffe should be privy to something kept secret from the Viceroy of India and yet pertaining so intimately to his charge. With understandable anger Mountbatten bursts into the billiards room and demands an explanation from Ismay. The simple 'Why did no one tell me?' elicits the unconvincing response, 'So you could better do your job.' Mountbatten is not convinced by Ismay's concern for future British interests in the Indian Ocean and the Middle East, and feels that he has been a pawn in a game captained by others. He accuses Ismay of having blood on his hands, only to be reminded that what has eventuated is, indeed, the 'Mountbatten Plan.'

In Karachi, to celebrate the birth of Pakistan, Mountbatten in an aside remarks to Jinnah that he got what he wanted. Jinnah, never satisfied, replies that he got only half of what he wanted, whereas the British got everything they were playing for; they are the real victors. Jinnah goes on to read a congratulatory letter from President Truman of the United States, prompting us, 70-odd years after the event, to reflect on that country's influence in South Asian affairs, along with Pakistan's military dictatorships, its unsuccessful wars with India, the loss of East Pakistan, the rise of radical extremism and the like. Mountbatten's words, 'There are no victors here', would seem to ring true.

It is easy to see Jinnah as the villain of the Partition, or the hero for those who saw the division as beneficial, but had the British perceived their future needs differently, there might have been good reason to doubt that the country would ever have been divided. However, Britain was indeed acutely wary of any means that might have allowed the Soviets to get the upper hand in the Indian Ocean and the Persian Gulf, and when Gurinder Chadha's Mountbatten tells Jinnah, 'It shouldn't be me standing here with you. It should be Churchill. He is the midwife who delivered your Pakistan', there is a strong suggestion that the idea of division contingent on the independence of India had enjoyed favour in London and that Mountbatten's predecessors in Delhi, Linlithgow and then Wavell, had played a significant role in cultivating that favour.

On the question of the ultimate responsibility for the division of India, each of the three films, *Gandhi*, *Sardar* and *Viceroy's House*, differs significantly from the others in its emphasis. While the two earlier films depict established views, Gurinder Chadha's film, being indebted somewhat to Narendra Singh Sarila's book, presents material previously not so well known that gives rise to a very plausible argument explaining the closeness of the British administration to the Muslim League and the rather hurried way in which the Partition of India was expedited. This was something that troubled the conscience of at least one man—Gurinder Chadha's Cyril Radcliffe.

Notes and References

1. *Viceroy's House* is also known as *Partition: 1947*. The former title is preferred here to avoid possible confusion with another film titled *Partition*, discussed later in this book.

2. The Rashtriya Swayamsevak Sangh (National Volunteer/Patriotic Organisation) is a militant right-wing extremist group, still functioning in India.

3. 14 August or Ramadan 27 in the Muslim calendar holds special significance for Muslims.

4. The Bengal famine occurred in 1943, but it was so cataclysmic that its ill effects lingered long.

5. Narendra Singh Sarila, *The Shadow of the Great Game: The Untold Story of India's Partition* (New Delhi: Harper Collins, 2005). The other book is Dominique Lapierre and Larry Collins, *Freedom at Midnight* (United States of America: Simon and Schuster, 1975).

two

The Absurd and the Unforeseen

Unbiased at least he was when he arrived on his mission,
Having never set eyes on the land he was called to partition
Between two peoples fanatically at odds,
With their different diets and incompatible gods.
"Time," they had briefed him in London, "is short. It's too late
For mutual reconciliation or rational debate ..."

Shut up in a lonely mansion, with police night and day
Patrolling the gardens to keep the assassins away,
He got down to work, to the task of settling the fate
Of millions. The maps at his disposal were out of date
And the Census Returns almost certainly incorrect,
But there was no time to check them, no time to inspect
Contested areas. The weather was frightfully hot,
And a bout of dysentery kept him constantly on the trot,
But in seven weeks it was done, the frontiers decided,
A continent for better or worse divided.

The next day he sailed for England, where he could quickly forget
The case, as a good lawyer must. Return he would not,
Afraid, as he told his Club, that he might get shot.

W. H. Auden, *Partition*

History, and W. H. Auden too, may have been a little unkind to Cyril Radcliffe. After all, it was not his decision to partition India. He simply responded to a summons to serve and did it as well as he could with the limited resources or support he had, and urged on by a most unreasonable time limit; and if the account in Gurinder Chadha's *Viceroy's*

House is to be accepted, he was to largely corroborate the work of a previous viceroy. Notably, he had the decency to refuse payment for his pains, apparently believing the task to have been unworthy. Indeed, the establishment of any partition in India could not have been consistently efficient and universally fair, let alone satisfactory to all. The effects of the Partition were largely unforeseen and what in fact might have been anticipated was not always met with a plan of action, sound or otherwise. There are a number of films which represent some of the aberrations and anomalies of the actuality of division, some of them amusing, some of them perplexing and some that can only make us gasp in wonder. In *Viceroy's House*, there is a scene in which Lord Mountbatten and Lord Ismay introduce Cyril Radcliffe to the task of rearranging the map of India. Radcliffe says, with apparent foresight of the absurd, 'You're asking me to draw a line through people's houses, rice and jute fields ....' Ismay agrees that the proposition might seem somewhat daunting and notes, 'We all accept that some anomalies will be inevitable.' Anomalies, indeed, there were.

Rajkahini

Srijit Mukherji's *Rajkahini* ('A Tale of the Raj', 2015) is set in a provincial brothel, which bursts out of its relative insignificance by becoming one of the 'inevitable anomalies' that Ismay had suggested might result from Radcliffe's endeavours, for his line dividing India's West Bengal from East Pakistan runs straight through the middle of the ladies' house. Two officials, Mr Sen representing the Congress and Mr Ilias representing the Muslim League, come to the brothel with the local police to serve an eviction notice to the madam, Begum Jaan, informing her that the building must be vacated within a month as check-posts are to be set up on the land on which it stands. Indeed, the Radcliffe Line is to be marked by a barbed wire fence running through the land occupied by the house and so the building has to be demolished to facilitate the erection of the fence. To clarify, Begum Jaan asks if the people standing on one side of the courtyard are in India and those on the other side are in Pakistan. Ilias gravely confirms this to be so. Begum Jaan looks stunned as her mind struggles to comprehend the weight of this verification, then suddenly she is convulsed with mirth, her laughter infecting all the other women and, probably, most of the audience too. Quite unable to see any humour in this, the official party remain po-faced, making the situation even funnier. At last, Begum Jaan's mirth subsides sufficiently to enable her to speak, declaring Radcliffe 'to be quite a weirdo if he has to hack the country like a butcher.' She describes, perhaps not entirely inaccurately, the partition blueprint as being 'amateurish' and 'half-baked'. Maintaining his dignity in the midst of this hilarity, Sen tries to persuade Begum Jaan of the seriousness of the situation and advises the Hindus and Muslims in her house to take themselves to the appropriate side of the border to avoid the likelihood of communal violence.

Begum Jaan's response is in accord with her political and social remoteness. She declares that whatever is decided in Delhi or Karachi is of no concern to her, Nehru and Jinnah are irrelevant, and even India and Pakistan are meaningless names, for her homeland is this building, a home where communal and caste distinctions have no significance for they have no place. As the laughter dissolves in passion for a tiny aspect of humanity, there now descends upon the action the chilling absurdity of the police aiming their weapons and the women raising their knives and choppers in a metaphorical suggestion of another kind of communal conflict. Like so many others who at the time of the Partition had fought, nobly or ignobly, to defend their homes, these women are similarly asserting their refusal to submit to a barbed wire fence. Eventually, however, like thousands of others they will become victims of the Partition and the indifference of its agents.

Shankhachil

The absurdity of the border is established at the beginning of Goutam Ghose's *Shankhachil* ('Boundless,'[1] 2016). In this film, the border separates India's West Bengal from Bangladesh, though it is the same border that was drawn by Radcliffe to separate India from East Pakistan. In a pre-titles sequence, a boat manned by four officers of the Bangladesh Rifles intercepts a boat bearing the Indian flag and carrying a party of simple Muslim rustics. They plead that they are going to a wedding on the other side of the border and promise to be back by the next morning. They are almost certainly genuine, but the Bangladesh Rifles officer cannot take any chances and the boat is turned around and sent back to the Indian side of the river. When asked by an accompanying journalist why he did not take stronger action, the officer points out that the rivers have been the lines of communication for these people for centuries, and only in the last 70 or so years since the Radcliffe Line was drawn has there been any need to police that communication. Obviously, potential infiltrators cannot simply be shot and there is by no means enough room in the jails to make arresting them an option either.

There is a cut to a group of people wading waist-deep through a jungle canal. As they come close to the camera, we see a few men, one carrying a ladder, and some boys, but most of the group are young women. They come out of the canal and stealthily make their way through the jungle. Later, after nightfall, we see them climbing the ladder, which is leaning against the barbed wire fence that marks the border, in order to get to the other side. In the process, a 14-year-old boy is shot dead by a member of the Indian Border Security Force (BSF). Here there is an indication of a very grim absurdity—protecting a border by shooting children. Another kind of absurdity intercuts the sequence of the group filing through the jungle and climbing over the fence after dark, and this is the celebration of exaggerated military pomp that is performed every day in the process of changing guards, raising and saluting flags, and sounding bugles. Such theatrical overplaying of simple formalities would seem to be a fatuous attempt to nationalistically ritualise the border and its protection in an endeavour to establish it as something patriotically iconic.[2]

An angry press contingent has come to demand answers from the BSF, whose officer, Ravi Verma, takes some of their questions. One of them indignantly alleges that the shooting was a 'major human rights violation' and Verma offers the curious response, 'It's our bloody history that's shot him,' quite cogently implying that the Radcliffe Line so many years earlier decided the fate of millions of innocent people. This notion that the Partition has imprisoned nations and people in the history that it created over the ensuing decades is certainly one that should bring into question the value that those lines on the map might ever have had. Verma goes on to describe the border as 'a forced Line of Control. It's not a border at all. It's absurd.'

The absurdity of this particular border is taken up by the other side. The Bangladesh Rifles officer whom we met at the beginning takes his journalist visitor along a part of the line and points out some of Ismay's 'inevitable anomalies'. He informs the journalist that the border runs for 4,095 kilometres, and that more than 1,100 kilometres of it runs through water. They enter a small village in which a mixture of Indians and Bangladeshis live, for here the line is not marked by a barbed wire fence because it runs through the middle of the village. (We are told that there are many such villages along the border.) Inside the village, on either side of a wide, muddy track, the officer points to a 'Bangladeshi cow' and some 'Indian goats'. Further down the track is a tattered white flag vaguely indicating the position of the border. We meet two neighbours chatting together; one's house is in India and his friend's house, just some metres away, is in Bangladesh. The officer points to a tall coconut tree, growing on a slight slant. He says that while its roots are in Bangladesh, the fruits fall in India. Finally, he shows the journalist a house, most of which is in one country but whose kitchen is in the other.

Shankhachil deals with the sad story of a 12-year-old girl from provincial Bangladesh who is seriously in need of heart surgery, and is taken by her parents to Calcutta for the operation. Before we reach that part of the narrative, however, there is the development of an idea that is very significant to the notions of 'partition' and 'border', and that idea concerns the primacy of notions such as 'ethos' and 'culture' in determining national identity,[3] notions which play a much more profound part in determining who we are than the borders that separate us from certain others. The shooting of the 14-year-old boy was out of inflated respect for a barbed wire fence; the death of little Rupsha in *Shankhachil* was most likely because her operation should have been performed earlier, and the reason that it was not was out of an inflated respect for the same barbed wire fence. The pre-Independence prophets of Partition gave rise to many cases of untold misery in not taking sufficiently into account the cultural and historical values that define a people, values that would seem to hold immensely more value than a fence.

In 1947 most people were optimistic that, terrible as it was, the violence could not last forever and things would settle down sooner rather than later. Indeed, the violence went on through Pakistan's wars of aggression against India[4] and flared through the Bangladesh War of 1971, resulting in Pakistan's loss of its eastern wing. Here, we will discuss two films that take up the theme of certain ramifications of the Partition playing themselves out after the event.

The two newly independent nations were just eight weeks old when Pakistan brought on its first war with India. The future of Kashmir, which is not absolutely certain even today, was very hazy at the time of the Partition. Pakistan tried to take advantage of the confusion and uncertainty and so started what is often known as the First Kashmir War (1947–1948).

The acrimony which peppered so much of Jinnah's rhetoric in agitating for a separate Muslim state and the extremes of violence that made the Partition such an infernal catastrophe ensured that instability would prevail in the subcontinent for decades to come. Indeed, of all the ill-effects of the Partition, this remains the most malignant.

Kya Dilli Kya Lahore

Vijay Raaz's 2014 film, *Kya Dilli Kya Lahore* ('What Delhi? What Lahore?') is set during this first Indo–Pakistan War and underlines, among many thought-provoking ideas, the abnormality of the war and the Partition from which it had emanated. Yet despite its context of military hostility, contrived jingoism and chest-thumping, *Kya Dilli Kya Lahore* is deeply rooted in simple notions of humanity.

There is a pre-titles sequence which fixes the film firmly in history. We see archival film footage featuring an excerpt from Nehru's famous 'At the stroke of the midnight hour' speech and the raising of the Indian tricolour, followed by the lofty language of Jinnah's speech on the foundation of Pakistan. The camera slowly moves down from Jinnah on a high podium to what initially looks like masses of people in his audience in the street below, but the picture is, in fact, file footage of a mass migration, at first through the streets of a city and then out on the open road. Here the narrator tells us that more than 2,500,000 went from Delhi to Pakistan and around same number went the other way. There is a reminder that the migration was not peaceful, as along with the pictures of long columns of displaced people there are also shots of arson and destruction, and there are the well-known pictures of the impossibly overcrowded trains.

The rolling of the opening titles is given added interest by the recitation of a poem in which the Radcliffe Line is likened to the lines of a *kabaddi*[5] court and the Partition to the playing of the game. The apparent absurdity of the comparison is an effective metaphor for the inanity of the division of the country.

> Let the line remain as it is.
> You come to my side and challenge me,
> smack my hand and run.
> I will catch you, hold you, pull your leg
> and not let you go back ...

A title card then gives us the time and place: '1948. North-West Frontier Province and Kashmir'. The camera panning over a desolate grassy area asserts a context of hostility as it passes over the bodies of two or three soldiers lying there. A soldier crawls towards the camera and almost immediately meets an officer, who orders the soldier to proceed to an Indian post to fetch a file on the plans for a tunnel to run from Delhi to Lahore. The hint of an absurdity emerges when one realises that the distance between Delhi and Lahore is in excess of 500 kilometres. One might also wonder why such an important file about something so extraordinary would be kept in a remote and meagre outpost as the one with which we will soon become familiar, and also that a Pakistani officer should have knowledge of it. The hint of absurdity is one of a number of pieces of grey if not black comedy which the director employs to prevent us from taking the military as seriously as it often takes itself, and to be at least a little suspicious of the politically-manufactured jingoism out of which so much hostility is derived.

At the Indian check-post, a soldier is talking on the radio to a superior, reporting that his comrades have not returned and that he is scared. His quite natural emotion invites hyperbole: 'A soldier is never alone. You have the whole of India with you.' And then:

> 'If you are afraid, why did you join the army?'
> 'I joined the army to cook. I am a cook.'
> 'Shut up!'

The Indian and the Pakistani soldiers meet each other at the well. The immense surprise of the Indian is marked by the dropping of his bucket and a shriek, startling the Pakistani, who almost falls into the well as the Indian runs away. The latter is genuinely scared and the former is apprehensive and wary. Both will be confined by these emotions for much of the film, adapting their behaviour to their own interpretations of the situation. They are anything but skilled warriors: the Indian holes up inside the small cottage that is the check-post and drops his rifle on the wooden floor; the noise surprises the Pakistani causing him to drop his rifle and making it go off. There is a clumsy attempt at communication, impeded by attempts—just as clumsy—to intimidate each other, an intimidation that is not even as skilful as it is sabre-rattling. The Pakistani talks tough about the number of people he has killed, and when the Indian lets out that he is a cook, the Pakistani declares that he was unnecessarily scared. His taunts make the Indian angry, and there is some indiscriminate firing which serves only to waste ammunition, although the Indian does sustain a wound to his upper left arm. There is mutual blaming, each accusing the other of the same things expressed as generalisations and clichés. Each adopts the official line of ascription of culpability, as though country is talking to country. The artifices of patriotism are being played out in the microcosm.

However, they start to see one another in less clichéd ways when they talk about their lives before the Partition. The Indian, who aims to live in Delhi after his family leaves the transit camp, grew up in Lahore; the Pakistani is originally from Delhi and now calls Lahore home. This correspondence of cities serves simply and effectively to minimise any differentiating suggestion that the words Indian and Pakistani might make, for their backgrounds have more to draw them together than to set them apart. The communication between the Indian, who will later become known as Samarth, and the Pakistani, who will become known as Rehmat Ali, takes on an increasingly human trend.

They talk about rains and the quality of crops, and the localities where each lived in Delhi and Lahore. There is shared nostalgia over the joys of the food in those cities and of the fun of flying kites. Rehmat remembers even the moon in Delhi with affection: 'Lahore's moon always snubbed me.' Samarth asks Rehmat about his family, and Rehmat tells him he has a wife, child and father.

'Mother?'
'You lot cut her to pieces.'
'Blood was shed on both sides.'
'A bit more on our side.'
'That's what everyone feels, brother.'

Having caught only brief glimpses of each other until now, the two men agree to reveal themselves to one another. As each takes in the look of the other, it is as though he is surprised to see a man and not a monster. But just as something positive might come of this realisation, a message comes over the radiotelephone reporting that the enemy has violated the ceasefire and many Indian soldiers have been treacherously killed; and so India declares Pakistan untrustworthy again and the two go back under cover.

A high shot of the check-post cogently emphasises the remoteness and isolation in which the two men have found themselves and each other. Although one is Indian, fighting for India, and the other is Pakistani, fighting for Pakistan, India and Pakistan might as well be on another planet. There is a touch of farce as they indulge in a bit of cat-and-mouse reconnaissance and find themselves inadvertently exchanging their positions. Samarth is heartened by the suspicion that Rehmat has run out of bullets and he kicks open the door of the cottage to ensconce himself inside it once again; Rehmat is just a slight jump ahead of him and Samarth is devastated to see the Pakistani's rifle inches from his head. There follows the ludicrous situation of Samarth making, at gunpoint, stuffed *paratha*s for Rehmat. This is all part of a creditable endeavour to destroy folly by laughing at it, the film making a valid point through its seemingly discordant comedy.

The scene shifts a little away from the cottage. Samarth is walking in front of Rehmat, carrying a large bundle of files. Samarth makes an important observation: 'Last night we were enemies. We aren't now.' Of course, it is questionable that they were ever enemies, but were only made to seem so by their uniforms. Hence, Otherness has no actuality but is simply made apparent by artifice; thus, it is questionable that mutual animosity is second nature to Indians and Pakistanis, despite the rancour emanating out of the Partition. It is nice to think of Samarth and Rehmat representing the majority, seeing value in simple human things rather than in negativity. However, the negative minority, in the form of a rustic postman, Barfi, who resents his lowly station and craves the glory of a military career, ambushes them. He has heard snatches of their friendly talk and uncovers the collection of files; he suspects Samarth of disloyalty and kicks him viciously. Mention of the stuffed parathas brings on even more ferocious blows from the would-be hero.

Barfi is a bully and, as will be seen later, far from a hero, but he is armed and the others are not, so he can stand over them. He assumes the status of an officer and makes Samarth salute him. Snarling, he calls Rehmat a Pakistani, which prompts Rehmat to protest that he lived 30 years—almost his entire life—in Delhi. The cynical, stupid postman misses the significant point that Rehmat is making, along with the implication that national identity in some cases may well be simply contrived. He sees Rehmat's protest as evidence of perfidy: 'You live in India for 30 years, then turn to them, join their army and now you are killing us.'

Again, comedy is employed, this time to expose the folly of men like Barfi. The postman is so startled by a frog that jumps out of Rehmat's bag that he drops his rifle in fright. Rehmat and Samarth quickly pick up the two rifles (Rehmat's and Barfi's) and aim at each other, with Barfi hiding behind Samarth. The moment of farce is carefully contained and the dialogue reverts to humane concerns. The postman remembers a letter he has for Samarth; it is from his father and is very familial. It also contains the news that Uncle Afzal, the father of Samarth's boyhood friend, Rizwan, has died. 'If tomorrow you face Rizwan, you won't be able to shoot him. We have kin on that side and this.' Again, enmity is ameliorated by long-lasting familiarity, and the amity between Samarth and Rehmat is also growing deeper. Samarth is ailing and needs water; Barfi is sent to get some, and Rehmat helps Samarth get up from the ground and seats him on a chair. There is some chat about their children and—at this late stage—Samarth asks Rehmat his name. Samarth falls off the chair and sprawls on the ground, and Rehmat runs to him, calling him 'brother'. The actuality of humanity is shown to be confronting the contrivances of patriotism.

The officer who had sent Rehmat Ali on this fool's errand now appears, determined to find the file he wants. The seemingly-dead Samarth stirs and Rehmat goes to him, calling him 'brother' again, which sends the officer into a rage. He beats Rehmat, then roughly shakes Samarth; he kicks him and aims his rifle at him, but before he can fire he is shot by Rehmat Ali. Brotherhood has defeated an absurd and hollow nationalism. However, nationalism re-asserts itself with a shot of soldiers' feet running through the long grass. Suddenly, Rehmat Ali is shot and he falls into Samarth's arms. Samarth cradles him and then starts wailing in profound grief.

The two cities of the title, Delhi and Lahore, bear fond appeal to both the protagonists. The two cities saliently bear evidence of the grandeur of Mughal tradition, although this is not mentioned in the film, where the aim is to focus on the mundane that gives men common ground. Ordinariness is highlighted to reduce constructs such as armies to simple common denominators. The film treats military matters almost with contempt, seeking the absurd and the hyperbolic by which to distract and guide the viewer into the fundamentally human world of family, home, work and leisure. Perhaps the most telling metaphor in the film is Samarth being obliged, at gunpoint, to cook for Rehmat. The Pakistani's upper hand is not as relevant as his expressions of gratitude and satisfaction at the stuffed parathas that it is the Indian's pleasure to prepare for a fellow soldier.

When the Partition was enacted, it is unlikely that many foresaw war between the two nations, and certainly not the persistent use of force on the part of either. Undoubtedly, no one in 1947 would have imagined a subcontinent dominated by two nuclear powers. And, with the rhetoric of the Two Nation Theory still fresh in their minds, no one would have imagined that Pakistan would lose its entire eastern wing in the war of 1971. The simple minds with which we might so readily sympathise in *Kya Dilli Kya Lahore* would seem to belong to a different—and saner—universe from the one accommodating the men who had assumed leadership after the Partition.

Bhaag Milkha Bhaag

Also concerned with the ramifications of the Partition playing themselves out in the subsequent years is Rakeysh Omprakash Mehra's *Bhaag Milkha Bhaag* ('Run, Milkha, Run', 2013). The film is about the life of the Indian international athletics champion, Milkha Singh, born on 20 November 1929[6] in the village of Govindpur which, in 1947, found itself in Pakistan. While the focus of the film is on his career in the army, with which he was able to combine his career as an athlete, there are flashbacks to the time of the Partition to show how that narrative emerged and how it conditioned his nature. The happy simplicity of his childhood is shown at the beginning, then his flight from the village, and then a time in a transit camp. The last 45 minutes of the film show in detail the circumstances leading to his flight and, 13 years later, his emotional return to his village. The denouement of the film is exceptionally moving.

The opening section depicts a young Milkha as the pride and joy of his family, not yet because of any athletic prowess but because he is believed to be destined for success in the world as he has learnt a few words of English. We see him going to the village school with his Muslim friend, a school where boys of all communities sit together under the watchful tutelage of a Sikh teacher. This whole section has hardly any germinal elements of narrative—indeed, it seems inconsequential—but it is, in fact, beautifully crafted to provide an intense contrast to the savagery that brings this sublime chapter in Milkha's life to an end as well as the feasibility of the emotions that unexpectedly prevail in the film's finale.

Milkha finds himself in a transit camp and, by a stroke of fortune, is reunited with his older sister. The struggle to survive hunger and hardship toughens Milkha, whose nature, it now appears, is to never submit to anything at all. He falls in with a shady group of boys who are greatly impressed by his strength and doggedness, and he is soon making money stealing coal from trains. It might seem that he is destined for a life as a petty crook, but a run-in with the law and the loving support of his sister turn him from delinquency to a career in the army, and it is here that he is recognised as a gifted athlete and is trained to literally take on the world.

There is one significant flashback that accounts for both Milkha's adamant refusal to visit Pakistan and then, having been persuaded to change his mind, his motivation to win there and overcome the entrenched demons of his past. It is shown first in an abbreviated form, primarily to make narrative sense of Milkha's subsequent flight across the border and his taking asylum in the transit camp. The full version of this flashback comes towards the end of the film. Earlier there is a scene of a heated discussion among the Sikhs of the village concerning what course of action would be most expedient for them to take. Some see evacuation as plain common sense; others are persuaded by the emotional appeal to their warrior tradition and the nobility of fighting for a just cause even when significantly outnumbered. As it is, they are too slow to act, and are caught in a raid by murderous Muslim horsemen. Seconds before his death, Milkha's father pleads, 'Run, Milkha, run!', thus giving another connotation to the title of the film.

Milkha does run, at first to safety, and then to personal fame and national glory. There is also a play on the word 'run' when Milkha competes at the Asian Games in Tokyo in 1958. There he meets for the first time his great Pakistani rival, Abdul Khalik, who says somewhat ambiguously, 'I heard that you had run from Pakistan ... and you've been running ever since.' Then a more sinister play on words is given in the context of the Rome Olympics, where Milkha fails to win a medal, losing ground by looking back. 'Why did he look back?', asks one perplexed commentator. There is an echo here of Milkha's father's injunction to run and not to look back. He does, however, look back at the exact moment when one of the butchers on horseback takes the old man's head off with his sword, thus creating an indelible image that will darken his psyche, at least until the glorious moments at the end of the film. We assume that the fugitive boy finds temporary shelter somewhere, for there is a simple cut to a shot of him returning later, calling for his mother. He finds the rest of his family, except his sister, slaughtered, thus providing another gruesome image to accompany the one which struck him when he looked back.

The last stages of the film bring together Milkha's Partition experience and his career as an athlete. Jawaharlal Nehru and his Pakistani counterpart, the military President Ayub Khan, have negotiated an India–Pakistan friendship games in Lahore in 1960. Nehru invites Milkha to lead the Indian team at those games. Milkha, however, is adamant in his refusal to visit Pakistan. It might be pointed out here that Milkha offers no sign of bigotry or communal acrimony. Rather, he is probably affected by a psychosis that makes him unable to confront the dreadful horror of his past. Whatever the psychology, it takes a giant like

Nehru to make him change his mind. But while everyone at the Games press conference is waiting for him to show up, Milkha revisits his old village.

We have an extended shot of him kneeling in front of his house, moved to tears. A small boy comes and gently offers him comfort; apparently recognising the face of the weeping man, the boy runs inside, and brings out a framed picture of Milkha on his blocks at the start of a race. Then Milkha's chubby school chum, some 13 years older, but still chubby, walks into the frame with tears running down his eyes, reciting the lines of a nonsense rhyme with which the boys amused each other when they were at school together. It is a highly emotional moment. Milkha has come to the country of the people who murdered his family and is received with immense affection and—as suggested by the framed picture—honour.

Milkha goes into the race of his life with these many different emotional experiences charging his motivation. He wins in spectacular fashion and receives generous praise from General Ayub, who dubs him the 'Flying Sikh'. However, of special significance is the scene in his village where loudspeakers are set up so that everyone may hear the broadcast of Milkha's race, and their rapturous delight in his victory is overwhelming. In these circumstances, at least, 'Indian' and 'Pakistani' are irrelevant. The villagers are elated because the victory went to *their* man. This is a persuasive philosophical context for the very emotional final scene in which Milkha, the champion, is seen to glory in the lap of honour, but he is accompanied by Milkha, the boy, who ran from Pakistan, still dressed in the same clothes he wore the day he fled his home. As he runs, he looks up to his adult counterpart, beaming with pride. One of the demons of the Partition would seem to have been exorcised.

The sporting narrative is significantly enhanced by the memory of Partition, which is a child's memory, perceived in bold, striking images rather than in an ordered narrative. But it is also a memory of a particular time, a time when families enjoyed simple pleasures together and took pride in their children learning English, for example; it was a time when boys of different communities went together to the same school; it was a time when they joked about reddening bums from a teacher's cane for a mischief as heinous as unpunctuality. It was an innocent era. Then came the Partition to destroy that innocence, the Partition in turn tarnishing its own gains with long-term shame and repressed guilt. *Bhaag Milkha Bhaag* offers no 'account' of the Partition; in the rustic simplicity of Govindpur, there are no indications of a looming cataclysm, no signs of even a burgeoning of antipathy of one community towards another. What is striking is the suddenness with which the Partition intrudes into the film. Like a bird of prey, it suddenly swoops into Milkha's consciousness, not as an introduction of a new narrative strand but as a very general indication of where Milkha is coming from and also as a signpost for the fuller treatment of the same memory later in the film, a memory which will emerge as an explanation of Milkha the man's conception of his place in the world as well as the motivation of Milkha the athlete. Nevertheless, the notion of suddenness bears significance beyond the understanding of an athlete's psyche. The desperation of the father in the 'Bhaag, Milkha, bhaag!' scene is linked to the suddenness of the confusion of the villagers a little earlier when they had become instantly embroiled in the 'flee or fight' controversy. There have been a couple of allusions to Milkha's incipient talent as a runner to make sense of his father imploring him to run; the old man knows well that he and the rest of his family have been caught unawares and that it is too late for them to save themselves, with the possible exception of Milkha. The imminent devastation will be succeeded by the long-drawn-out trauma experienced by those who were able to flee the slaughter of loved ones, as well as the trauma experienced by those whose dominance permitted them to stay, though bearing the guilt and the shame that went with it. *Bhaag Milkha Bhaag* is indeed an excellent story of an athlete and a national hero, but it is also unavoidably the story of a people's tragedy.

Viceroy's House revisited

In a divorce there should be an equitable property settlement; in the case of the Partition of India, Pakistan had to have some material assistance merely in order to function. While the division of the population would be effected on a largely voluntary basis and the division of the land seemed to be feasible at least, there were assets that it was not possible to divide. These were the 'unique institutions'—printing presses, mints, ammunition factories, hospitals, laboratories, libraries, research institutes and the like, which would be rendered useless to both sides if they were actually divided. *Sardar* considers this problem without cinematic lustre, concisely, simply and clearly, through unelaborated essential dialogue around the Viceroy's table. Patel is magnanimous in offering the sharing of such institutions until Pakistan is able to set up its own. As for Jinnah's demand that the Intelligence Bureau be divided, Patel's reply is simple: 'The country may be divided, its secrets cannot be. After Partition the Intelligence Bureau's work will only increase.' Pakistan would have to look after itself in this regard. Mountbatten had already declared that until all matters regarding the Partition had been resolved, the army should remain under the control of the British government. Jinnah's demand that a Pakistan army be formed and in place by 15 August is agreed to, but Patel does not agree to Pakistan taking a share of the Air Force. 'We'll not aid Pakistan in killing our Baluchistan and Pathan brothers.' The most significant of Jinnah's demands was for a direct split of the cash reserves totalling about 2,000 million rupees. Patel points out that a 50-50 division would be an oversimplification, as things such as population and area have to be taken into consideration. Jinnah insists that 1,000 million rupees would be essential to tide the new country over the current financial year, and after a whisper from his aide, Patel agrees to hand over 750 million, 20 now and 55 after all the accounts have been settled. Later we will see this as being Gandhi's last major controversy, for Pakistan launches an attack in Kashmir hardly before the year is ended, and Nehru and Patel, not unreasonably, refuse to pay the balance of 550 million to have it used to finance an aggression against India. Gandhi stands up for principle: a promise is a promise and must be kept. He embarks on the last fast of his life and the money is paid.

In *Viceroy's House*, the property settlement is imbued with a touch of the absurd. Mountbatten tells his assembled domestic staff that the national assets and debt would be distributed 80 per cent to India and 20 per cent to Pakistan. We then witness some aspects of the division. The dining room must provide 15 cases of soup spoons to India and three to Pakistan; 40 cases of teaspoons to India and 10 to Pakistan; and 20 cases of butter knives to India and five to Pakistan. The band retains a tuba but surrenders a French horn. The library in India manages to keep the Brontes and Jane Austen, but is in a fix regarding the sharing of encyclopaedias, 20 per cent of which must go to Pakistan. Should the new nation get A to E or S to Z? Other films show that the quaint anomalies were greatly outnumbered by the wholesale loss of property and livelihood, loss of loved ones and the loss of life. To the millions of humble, dislocated people, the Radcliffe Line imposed losses far more serious than embossed cutlery, leather-bound books and foreign musical instruments.

Garm Hawa

One of the great flaws in the partition formulation was engendered by the serendipity thinkers who saw a divided India much like a mathematical equation: draw lines here and there and have Muslims live on one side and Hindus—and anyone else who cares to—live on the other, and all will live happily ever after, for there will be no more bickering, no more communal strife, and no more majoritarian bullying. In M. S. Sathyu's 1974 Partition cinema classic, *Garm Hawa* ('Hot Winds'), following hard on the opening titles is a photograph of Mahatma Gandhi at the moment of his assassination. While a might-have-been, too terrible to contemplate, had been obviated when it was learned that the great man had been killed by a Hindu fanatic and not by a Muslim, Sathyu's use of this photograph right at the beginning of his film is a metaphorical suggestion that with the death of the prophet of Hindu–Muslim amity, that great ideal would now be immensely harder to achieve. Indeed, a serendipity thinker might have been dumbfounded at the plight of one Muslim family for whom the Partition was by no means simple, but rather led to an inescapable descent into penury and heartache.

The narrative deals with the Mirzas, an extended family in Agra, whose fortune is founded on shoe manufacturing. The head of the family is Halim, an activist in Muslim politics, successful businessman and inveterate egotist. Goaded by self-interest and an inflated sense of his own importance, he decides to take his immediate family to Pakistan. His younger brother, Salim, opts to remain in India along with his own immediate family and the ancient *mater familias*. Most of the rest of the film depicts the pressures that cause Salim to question the good sense of that decision.

While riots, with attendant rape, pillage, murder and destruction were prominently efficacious in urging members of the minority community to flee to the alternative state, violence plays only an isolated role—though indeed a persuasive one—in swaying Salim's thinking. Salim is eventually led to feel quite unwelcome in the land of his birth and his forefathers, but the forces that make that discomfort manifest are mostly of an economic and political nature. The first reason behind the discomfort concerns the right to property. The family home had been bequeathed to Halim, but the factory in which the family's fortune was made was inherited by Salim. The house is a large and valuable one, big enough to comfortably accommodate such an extended family. Salim hopes that his brother might transfer the ownership to him, and it is vital that this be done quickly, for if it is not done within a certain time the government will claim the house as abandoned property. Ultimately, time runs out without Halim being able to think beyond his own concerns and bring himself to India for a few days to sign the relevant papers; the house passes into the government's hands and is sold off (to a very sympathetic merchant in the shoe business), and Salim and his family and elderly mother are obliged to find rental accommodation. The old lady finds it particularly painful to leave her home of so many years.

In trying to resurrect the family business, Salim needs to borrow money, but here lies another seemingly impossible hurdle: banks are not willing to lend money to Muslims. It is a matter of financial institutions protecting their own interests by minimising their risks. How can the bank manager be sure that Salim, if granted the loan, will not take the money and run to Pakistan, never to repay it? Of course, the house might have been mortgaged—but that was another uncleared hurdle. Salim meets the same problem when looking for rental accommodation, as prospective landlords are reluctant to enter into agreements with people likely to run off, dishonouring the lease. Indeed, one prospective landlord demands a year's rent paid in advance.

Salim had at one time been a successful and reputable businessman of the city, but now his business and his reputation both go into decline. Officialdom, influenced by the new Partition-related regulations and conditions, plays a large part in this decline, but so too does Salim's own conservative outlook. Even more significant are the personal trials faced by his children, Amina and Sikander, trials that are very closely related to the new realities brought out by the Partition.

For a long time Amina and Halim's son, Kazim, had been very close and their marriage seemed certain, at least until

Kazim goes to Pakistan with his parents. He promises to return to India to take Amina back to Pakistan as his wife, and Amina remains faithful to him while she waits. In the meantime she is wooed by another cousin, Shamshad, whom she spurns at every opportunity out of loyalty to Kazim. It becomes apparent that there is no likelihood of Halim returning to Agra and so the prospect of Amina's marriage with the boy she loves grows dim, but one night Kazim arrives at the house unannounced. He tells Amina that his father wants him to marry the daughter of a Pakistani politician and that he has been awarded a scholarship to study in Canada. It is his plan to marry Amina and then take up the scholarship. Here again, officialdom gets in the way. It is understandable that those who have elected to go to Pakistan should still think familiarly of the home they left behind, but in fact Pakistan and India are foreign to one another, each demanding of the other's citizens formalities such as passports and registration with the local police. Kazim, in maintaining secrecy from his father, comes without a passport and fails to report to the police. He is arrested, escorted to the border and sent back to Pakistan. That is the end of Amina's dream of marriage with him. However, Kazim's place is quickly taken by Shamshad and Amina develops a deep affection for him, but that too is stifled when he goes to Pakistan with his father, promising to send his mother soon to fetch Amina. The mother does return to Agra to shop for her new daughter-in-law's trousseau, but it turns out that the new daughter-in-law is not Amina. Heartbroken, Amina breaks her parents' hearts by committing suicide.

Salim must also suffer the melancholy of watching his graduate son, Sikander, trying to find work in a job market which, it seems, is less than sympathetic towards Muslims. Ignoring the fact that India is a secular state, employers tend to subscribe to the philosophy that while there are jobs for Muslims in Pakistan, why should Muslims be given Hindus' jobs in India?

Ultimately Salim starts to realise that merely to remain in India might be dangerous. One day a tight squeeze in the narrow road through the market cannot quite successfully be negotiated by the driver of the *tonga* in which he is travelling and it tips over, the vehicle clipping a fruit vendor's stand, spilling his merchandise all over the road. Tempers are frayed, violence erupts, and soon a wholesale riot rages. A stone is thrown, hitting Salim on the head, and the maddened mob goes on to set fire to his factory. Then, as though this is not enough for one man to bear, a charge of espionage is brought against him arising from his sending out the plans of the ancestral property to his brother in Pakistan. Here is an indication of the paranoia that was starting to corrode relations between the two newly-created states. The charge is quickly discredited and Salim is acquitted, but his reputation is sullied nevertheless and now he genuinely feels that he cannot go on.

Salim is conservative by nature. His earlier success in business would seem to have overshadowed any resolve to move with the times, preferring to leave himself and his future in the hands of God. He is quite unprepared for the changing times, especially the new changes that are particularly pertinent to Muslims. Despite his unwillingness to leave the land of his birth and his strength in accepting somewhat fatalistically the buffets of a changing India, the downward spiral in his life eventually becomes too much for him to counter any longer the reasoned arguments for migrating to Pakistan.

The film has an extraordinary ending. While Salim and his family are on their way to the station, their tonga is held up by a large demonstration of disaffected workers, many of them comrades of Sikander. Wanting to join them in solidarity, the boy gets down from the tonga with Salim's encouragement. After a few moments' thought, Salim, belying his conservatism and passivity, is also drawn to the fight for change. Perhaps his gesture seems extravagant, but beyond the realism of the moment it is an indication that conservatism is antithetical to progress—indeed, for Salim it has been antithetical even to the continuance of the status quo—and change must be embraced. It is also a recognition of the fact that more significant than the communal divide in the new India is the class divide.

Garm Hawa is a moving human document, a telling account of distress engendered by a series of unforeseen setbacks. The riot, realistically depicted as it is, does not produce the same visceral pain as, for example, the safeguards initiated by the banks. It is the relentlessness of these usually subtle setbacks that eventually persuades Salim to opt for Pakistan, and it is the self-evident pertinence of a non-communal challenge that persuades him to remain in India.

Lord Ismay, in *Viceroy's House*, could never have imagined the depth of understatement in his words, 'We all accept that some anomalies will be inevitable.' Many of the anomalies were also absurdities. Indeed, emblematic in its absurdity is the notion of the Radcliffe Line, like a noble steed charging into the fray and blinkered against any lateral distraction, forging its ever-onward push straight through the middle of a mofussil brothel. The more mundane incongruities that we see in the border village visited in the beginning of *Shankhachil*, summed up by the angular coconut tree with its roots in one country and dropping its fruit in the other, must be impressive in number and variety and must have welded their discrepancies into the evolved ordinariness of daily life in many rural areas. The detail in the post-Partition property settlement in *Sardar* and *Viceroy's House*, especially the latter, might seem fatuous when, with the concern for the proper division of such things as silver cutlery, we remember the millions who lost everything they had spent their entire lives working for.

The Partition, however, was much more than property and cartographical fine detail; it was one of the most catastrophic human disasters of all time. The somewhat grim comedy that characterises *Kya Dilli Kya Lahore* is indeed fitting as the context for the unnatural actuality that is basic to that film. The two central characters were both born in the same country; one had left Delhi to go and live in Lahore and one had left Lahore to go and live in Delhi. Now, because of a new line on the map, they are enemies and might well achieve honour by killing one another. Here the absurdity is the brittle nationalism that supports a concocted patriotism. Belonging is taken a step further in the last parts of *Bhaag Milkha Bhaag*, where Milkha's erstwhile fellow villagers, who have kept his memory alive with a framed photograph, rejoice wholeheartedly in *their man* winning the race which *their countryman* was supposed to win. In this case, nationalism is irrelevant. In *Garm Hawa*, the unforeseen obstacles with which the partition-in-practice buffets the Mirza family are enough to send them belatedly to Pakistan, yet are ultimately subordinated to greater notions of equity and their own perceived sense of belonging. Here, social justice emerges greater in importance than national sentiment.

Notes and References

1. 'Shankhachil' actually means the Brahminy kite.
2. In other films even sillier performances are depicted on the western border at Wagah.
3. This is discussed in more detail in Chapter 7.
4. In 1947, 1965, 1971 and 1999, as well as lesser hostilities.
5. A traditional Indian team contact sport that involves 'raiding' and 'capturing'.
6. Most references give this as his date of birth; Britannica.com gives it as 17 October 1935. Thus, in 1947 he would have been either 18 or 12 years old. In this film, Milkha as a boy looks much closer to 12 years than to 18. The major international sporting events that were pinnacles in his career should also be taken into account in determining his date of birth.

three

Chinnamul
A Case Study in Dislocation

The Partition of India was decided on and enacted in great haste. Those whom it would most radically affect were neither consulted nor adequately informed or forewarned about what new directions their country was being obliged to take. Under a heavy blanket of ignorance, superstition was fostered and violence spread unchecked. When the Partition was decreed, the danger in the air led many people to perceive an urgency which in turn led to more haste and panic in seeking safety and security somewhere far away from what they had always known as home.

There are those who would want to persuade us of the somewhat facile belief that the Partition was enacted in acknowledgement of the 'truth' of Jinnah's Two Nation Theory.

> The Hindus and Muslims belong to two different religious philosophies, social customs, literatures. They neither intermarry nor interdine together and, indeed, they belong to two different civilizations which are based mainly on conflicting ideas and conceptions.[1]

Estimates of the soundness or otherwise of the theory vary greatly. Whether or not interdining and intermarriage are essential aspects of a national polity may be questioned. There is, for example, considerable evidence in Tanvir Mokammel's documentary, *Simantarekha* ('The Borderline', 2015), of inter-communal sharing on the occasion of religious festivals, a socio-cultural phenomenon that is also illustrated in Tareque Masud's *Matir Moina* ('The Clay Bird', 2002). While the politics of division might be chattered about by a minority of urban intellectuals, the realities of rural labour did little to generate communal differentiation among the masses whose livelihood depended on the land and the waters. In Nimai Ghosh's *Chinnamul* ('The Uprooted', 1950), we are presented with the rural people of East Bengal, who are largely ignorant about the proposal to partition their country and who are by no means corroded by communal dissension.

Chinnamul is notable for the fact that it was made in 1950, making it one of the earliest films on the Partition and contemporaneous with the migrations that had begun several years earlier and were still going on. On a more superficial level, it features a later luminary of Indian cinema, Ritwik Ghatak, as a member of its cast and as an assistant director.[2]

Some seven decades after its release, Nimai Ghosh's landmark film comes across as somewhat dated, even a little quaint. Much of its dialogue seems to have been improvised, while its acting, particularly its free use of gratuitous gesturing, betrays a theatrical influence reminiscent of the style of the famous Indian People's Theatre Association founded in 1943.[3] The effect of filmed theatre is also suggested by so much that is shot inside a studio. Nevertheless, the film has its genuine strengths: particularly, we might note the quality of its outdoor cinematography, which is truly remarkable both in presentation and in imagery, as well as the sharp, concise communication of its story. The story embraces a simple venture of a group of people persuaded in an atmosphere of profound apprehension to leave their homes and start a new life elsewhere. What enriches this minimal narrative is the account that emerges irrepressibly of people—we see hundreds of them, representing hundreds of thousands more—and their suffering, which ultimately lends epic proportions to this human story that below the surface is anything but simple.

Immediately following the opening titles, a title card tells us that *Chinnamul* is not the product of any political interest, nor does it take issue with any individual or group, but that 'This film is a stark portrait of the lives and struggles of the victims of Partition.' Indeed, the people on whose lives and struggles the film focusses are Hindus, yet their Hinduism is marked by only one allusion, and that is Haran's mother's wish to bathe in the Ganges when they reach Calcutta; moreover, this wish is presented more for the light comic effect it might have rather than with an intention to suggest piety of a particular religiosity. Ghosh has been careful to portray his refugees without evident communal distinction, thus imbuing them with the broadest possible human appeal.

The card then goes on to identify the people as coming from 'Naldanga, a sleepy village in East Bengal.' With a touch of what seems almost like naiveté, the card says, 'Even this small village could not escape the blasts and waves of time.' Indeed, no village, small and insignificant or prominent and imposing, could escape the turbulence of such a seemingly random cataclysmic blow as the Partition of India. *Chinnamul* makes clear, in a deceptively simple way, that ordinary humble people were, in fact, those most prone to its devastation.

The opening shots are emblematic of East Bengal, an exceptionally riverine region. We first see a vast river and a large four-oared boat being rowed from the right side of the frame to the left; we then see a smaller boat in a narrower stream, followed by an extended shot of the waters of a river lapping at its banks. There is no narrative significance in this, the point being simply to locate a general region and suggest something about its peculiar lifestyle. A simple architectural juxtaposition suggests the social co-existence of two prominent religious communities, their longevity in this region being evident in the apparent condition of the buildings. Shots of the fields indicate agriculture and a shot of a potter at his wheel denotes traditional crafts. The overall impression is one of tradition, simplicity and serenity.

However, the rustic charm is belied by the reality of hardship. The artisan making a comb for the protagonist Srikanta's wife mentions difficult times, and Srikanta corroborates this by telling him that he lost half of his land in the terrible famine of 1943, the effects of which were still being felt in some parts of Bengal four years later.[4] What little he has left is barely sufficient to feed his family. Along with the pleasantness of birdsong being heard over the glimpses of rural life, there is also a mention that jute prices are expected to plummet.[5] These scenes of rustic serenity, with snippets of dialogue suggesting hardship of one kind or another, are transformed by the shots of a storm brewing. The camera focuses on a bird, its nest in a tree that is bending in the strong wind. The bird will surely weather the storm, but many people will not be able to survive the tempest that is blowing up in the affairs of men. (The story opens during the monsoon not long before the Partition, so the shots of the storm bear a sense of verisimilitude, but their simple symbolic value should not be overlooked. The poetic intent in this will become manifest a little later.)

A village fair offers a passing element of happiness, but even this is tempered by Srikanta's discussion with some other men about what would seem to be an impending disaster. One of them declares that in unity there is strength, but the forces of disunity would seem to have the upper hand. There is talk of the British leaving India and the country being partitioned, but some are incredulous at the thought: 'Is the country a lump of flesh that it could be cut in half?'

Then Srikanta is warned of a conspiracy against him: an unlikely bond exists between a Hindu, Madhu Ganguly, and a Muslim, Muzaffar Khan, who, despite their communal differences, are partners in crime. During the famine four years ago, Srikanta caught them smuggling rice, and they have not yet forgotten the consequences of that. Now they are conniving to take revenge on Srikanta and through their connections with corrupt elements among the police they contrive to have him arrested on false charges and locked away for a time.

This wickedness has a profound effect on Srikanta's devoted wife, who is expecting their first child. There is a scene in which we see her detached and melancholy. She looks nostalgically around their little cottage and envisions a baby in a basket and Srikanta dandling it. The vision fades, she is glum again, and the scene concludes with a shot of her sleeping alone. We should not miss the value of the essential ordinariness of what, in fact, is the dream of every would-be parent.

Ghosh is intent on building up his storm. Dark clouds gather, thunder is heard, the river swells and the rain comes down. Trees bend in the gale and the waters surge, and these shots are superimposed over shots of people in agitation—meetings, microphones and impassioned speakers. There are utterances of 'Pakistan' and 'Hindustan'. Houses burn and newspaper headlines cry out the imminent division of Bengal.

There is an interesting twist to the popular history here. The Hindus start to feel that they cannot stay back, but it is not so much their Muslim neighbours who are pushing them out, but the cunning and contriving men—Muslim and Hindu—with the power that comes with money. Indeed, it is Madhu Ganguly who advises the Hindus of Naldanga to leave, warning them of serious trouble that might be only a few days away, and while this might be a figment of his connivance, there are indications that he might also be right. For the sake of their lives they must sell everything and leave. 'Must sell' is to be taken literally, and because selling is more urgent for the vendor than purchasing is for the buyer, it also means that everything will go for a song. Property that is not easily portable must be sold, and for much less than it is worth, and immovable property—land and houses—will go to men like Madhu Ganguly for next to nothing. There are shots of Madhu and Muzaffar measuring land, and then we see Madhu persuading some remaining villagers that they too must leave, for their village and some nearby villages are already empty or quite depleted. He advises them to go to Calcutta, from where he has recently returned, and tells them on 'good authority' that the government has made all the right arrangements for them there. They believe him.

The human side of the upheaval is reflected in shots of people packing what few belongings they can take with them—which means pulling up deep-planted roots and wrenching oneself from what has been home to generations of one's family. There is also the unwanted pressure. Srikanta's wife is approached by Madhu Ganguly, who is keen on purchasing their house, but she refuses to sell it without her husband's approval. With Srikanta locked up in jail, Bishuda assumes leadership of the fleeing group of Naldanga villagers, and is at once concerned for Srikanta's pregnant wife and for Haran's elderly mother who 'will have to be carried on our shoulders.' Srikanta's wife does not want to go anywhere until her husband returns, but it would be very dangerous for her to remain in a deserted village, especially with predators like Madhu Ganguly lurking about. At last, goodbyes are said and the long journey starts, first to the ferry, then to the railway station and then onto the train that will take them to Calcutta. The train journey extends overnight and well into the next day, and is clearly uncomfortable. People are seen sitting on the floor, while some are obliged to stand as there is not enough room to accommodate everyone in even the most basic semblance of comfort. We might, however, bear in mind the countless hordes who had no access to trains and who covered hundreds of dangerous miles on foot.

A crowded train is seen coming into Calcutta's Sealdah Station. It is not one of the fabled Partition trains with people hanging from the doors and windows and covering the roof, but it is overly full, nevertheless. The crowded train is complemented by the crowds covering the station concourse and the platforms, sitting, sleeping, eating—simply living. There is a shot of a little boy asleep on the ground and of a naked baby lying on a mat, crying, probably in hunger. The faces of the women of the Naldanga group show their dismay as they are confronted with this distressing reality of dislocation. The new arrivals see a broad picture of hopelessness and helplessness. A long shot of the concourse shows people camped there, while others are seen trying to move through them and their bedding and cooking arrangements. Bishuda and the other men from Naldanga get into a conversation with some people who have preceded them, learning that they have been there for a fortnight already, without any hint of finding anywhere better to go. The conditions are clearly too dreadful even for a night or two, and one of the men says ruefully that it was a mistake to have come here. For some of the women, there is the ever-present danger of unwanted interest from men outside their group. All the refugees are quietly fraught with worry about a bleak, uncertain future. And then there is an announcement that plague and cholera have broken out and that everyone should get themselves inoculated.

The focus returns to Srikanta's wife who is dreaming of her home and her husband. She, like so many others, is a long, long way from both. She yearns to go back to Srikanta, and Haran's mother longs for her home, as does a friend who cannot stand this insufferable place. But home has already changed irrevocably; there is a cut to a shot of pariah dogs outside a deserted cottage and a bearded Srikanta—visually enhancing the notion of change—comes to the door of what was his house and tells someone that he will leave for Calcutta immediately. In the meantime, the Naldanga men locate a large, vacant house and they all set off for it. There is a shot of Srikanta on the train, and then another of him coming out of the main entrance of the Sealdah Railway Station, but finding his wife and friends is now going to be very difficult.

There is a cut to a shot of the swarms on the Sealdah concourse, a close shot of a woman cooking, and another of naked toddlers crawling about. Srikanta enquires at a non-governmental organisation (NGO) desk, but no help is forthcoming. He looks around inside the station and learns that they have all left for a house, but no one knows where it is located. He comes out into the sea of people that is Calcutta, and a rooftop shot of the city makes it clear that it is a world away from his village.

A little earlier one of the men who had been waiting for a fortnight at Sealdah had told the Naldanga men, 'Calcutta is an odd city with odd people. Nobody seems to care.' We now see evidence of this as the owner of the house the group have come to turns up and orders them out, demanding that they leave within a week. He is indeed quite bereft of compassion. Of course, when a problem seems too great to resolve, many people harden their hearts and profess that it is not their concern. However, there are many examples, particularly well-documented in Tanvir Mokammel's *Simantarekha*, for example, of ordinary people going to extraordinary lengths to help the refugees from what had become Pakistan.

There are several sequences showing Srikanta, barefoot, wandering the streets of the great metropolis, looking for his wife and friends. He makes enquiries but all of them are fruitless. His task is not impossible, but he will need luck, something that the film is well-equipped to provide. In reality, many people in similar situations went on looking for weeks, months, even years. Many never found the ones they were looking for.

The Naldanga refugees face another problem—the lack of work. Unemployment was one of the most common trials displaced people had to face, but there was also the pain in making do with work that denoted a distinct drop in status from what one had been used to. To depict this, we have the craftsman who took such care, and time, in making combs in the village now reduced to hawking mass-produced combs on the streets of the city. Then dissensions within the group develop as the hawker of combs is caught hoarding his money rather than pooling it for group's common use. There is also a sense of shame among the men that they depend on the income brought in by the women, who earn a little money by making paper bags from old newspapers.

The luck that Srikanta needed has now been provided by Ghosh. We see more shots of him wandering the streets of the city, but we learn that someone from the group has spotted him. We also learn that a little earlier his wife had gone into labour. The doctor, who has delivered a baby boy, declares both mother and son to be in need of specialist care—truly an ominous pronouncement under these circumstances. However, Srikanta finds them at last, and his wife is blissfully happy. She just wants to go back to the village and set up home as a family. In the commotion that follows—the promotion of further uncertainty by the owner, who brings thugs armed with lathis to evict the squatters—Srikanta's lovely wife dies. The thugs become quiet at Bishuda's plea that they listen to reason, but do not leave. The final shot is of Srikanta holding his motherless baby son in his arms, looking apprehensively into an uncertain future, his face superimposed over the opening shot of an East Bengal river and a boat, to which happiness, we may assume, he will never return.

In later chapters and in different contexts, the notion of dislocation will become apparent in various ways. The depiction of dislocation given in *Chinnamul* is by no means comprehensive or definitive, nor does it set out to be overly dramatic or seek to exaggerate the suffering experienced by most refugees—if anything, the suffering is underplayed. The film is valuable, however, for its simple and somewhat stark account of the circumstances, leaving the viewer to grapple with unanswered questions. When was the Sealdah Station eventually cleared of the refugees camping there? How many people died on the station? How many went missing? How big a problem was the immoral recruitment of women from among the refugees? Was the landlord's gang of thugs a common phenomenon? Did this gang complete the work it set out to achieve?

We might wonder at the ending of the film. Certainly, without the Partition and the need to flee their home, the woman's confinement would have been much less difficult and she would have been supported by her husband rather than constantly worrying about him day and night. However, given the circumstances, both physical and emotional, death in childbirth must have been not uncommon among penniless refugees in the first half of the last century. What is of interest in Ghosh's ending to his film is the posing of a challenge to Srikanta to bring up his motherless son in the somewhat hostile environment, as suggested by the threat of the landlord and his thugs, and the earlier references to popular indifference. The abandonment of home under any circumstances would have been painful enough, but the removal from a remote village to a bustling metropolis, without any prospects, must have been an overwhelming nightmare.

There are indeed countless nightmare narratives experienced by people dislocated by the Partition. Some suffered more intensely than others, some suffered longer, but the suffering was real and it left its scars. For us today looking back on that tragic time, what makes the suffering more pitiable is the fact that it was often generated by ruthless acquisitive rogues seeking to profit at the expense of the helpless, unprepared and ill-informed. It would be nice to think that the likes of Muzaffar Khan and Madhu Ganguly were chastened by justice, but it is very likely that they died peacefully in their beds, leaving a nice legacy for their heirs, while Srikanta and his son .... But that film has not been made yet.

Notes and References

1. Presidential address by Muhammad Ali Jinnah to the Muslim League Lahore in 1940.

2. Some of Ghatak's films, on the nostalgia generated by the Partition, are discussed in Chapter 7.

3. Ghosh had in fact begun his career with Utpal Dutt's Little Theatre Group.

4. The Bengal famine claimed the lives of at least three million people through starvation and disease.

5. East Bengal was the world's biggest supplier of jute.

four

Uprooted and Lost

One of the saddest outcomes of the Partition was the darkening of the lives of innumerable people due to the fracturing of families and friendships. Some separations were voluntary, where some elected to remain 'at home' while others chose to go and make a new home in the other country, but it would seem that a very great number of separations were imposed by unexpected circumstances. Given the urgency of flight that was often brought about by the violent turmoil that threatened mere survival, getting lost in the crowd must have been a common occurrence. Serious injuries were sustained and lives were lost without a family member or friend being aware. Many separations were the result of deliberate abductions, usually of women; in time, many such women were restored to their community, though there were very many who were not so lucky. Surviving such a catastrophe was not like simply changing one's address. The Partition of India brought about the biggest mass migration in history, dislocating some 14 million people. The number of lives lost in the chaos may have been as many as two million. Like every colossal human tragedy, the Partition too has given rise to innumerable heartrending stories, and also inspired some extraordinary ones; cinema has embraced both, and more.

Chhalia

Made a little more than a decade after Independence, the alienation caused by the Partition forms the narrative basis of Manmohan Desai's *Chhalia*[1] (1960). It soon becomes evident, however, that the fact of the Partition is little more than a convenient plot mechanism. *Chhalia* is by no means a bad film, but it is nevertheless a Hindi cinema stock-in-trade, giving us a melodrama of estrangement, search, misunderstanding and re-estrangement, and eventually, reconciliation through the noble agency of a selfless saint from the slums.

The film opens with Kewal's marriage to Shanti, and their wedding night is celebrated in Lahore while the city burns. The lights inside their house suddenly go out and he tells her that the lights burning outside are 'the lights of darkness. Entire Lahore is burning today. Men have become beasts'. He offers this observation in much the same way as one might pass an opinion on the weather. The narrative then jumps forward five years and we learn that Kewal and his father left Lahore, as did Shanti's parents and her brother, soon after the riots began. Apparently no one thought of taking Shanti along nor did anyone enquire after her in all that time. We might infer something from her father's statement later that after she married Kewal, Shanti was no longer his daughter but a part of her in-laws' family. Moreover, because she had lived as an unmarried woman all those years, her family, fearing dishonour, had given out to all who asked that Shanti was dead. Now that charade had to be maintained. Kewal soon finds her and his attitude is more promising, until Shanti presents him with his son, who was born some time after his father left for India. The boy introduces himself as Anwar, and Kewal, appalled at the Muslim name, is immediately overwhelmed with an irrational suspicion about his wife that cannot be dispelled because he is too pompous to allow her the right of giving him a full explanation. By now it is clear that the Partition is not in the foreground of the film's narrative or philosophical interest, but that *Chhalia* is more concerned with cruel and outdated patriarchal Hindu social values.

Gadar: Ek Prem Katha

Anil Sharma's film, *Gadar: Ek Prem Katha* ('Rebellion: A Love Story', 2001), was a great box office success, and it does indeed meet a number of the criteria of a Bollywood blockbuster: it has at its core an exceptionally good story, it is well-acted, and it is a visual delight, often quite spectacular. The songs, given that we have to have them, are splendidly directed and greatly enhance the film's appeal as entertainment; similarly, the fights are ingeniously choreographed and are, literally, incredible. However, as a serious representation of the Partition, *Gadar* fails, largely because of the elements that make it spectacular entertainment. The excellent story is compromised by the urge to entertain that throws into the mix items of narrative that could be done without and flab that is extraneous to the core narrative, including sequences of irritatingly unfunny comedy. The film also runs on for a little under three hours; indeed, just the train sequence at the end, with all its miraculous violence, takes up nearly 20 minutes.

Pressed by the dire threat of communal riots, a wealthy businessman, Ashraf Ali, and his family are urged to leave Amritsar for Lahore. Shots of stations and trains in *Gadar* are remarkably realistic and the viewer can get quite overwhelmed by the surging masses of people. As the train is about to leave, the urgency to get on board is also touched with panic. Ashraf Ali's daughter, Sakina, stumbles in the melee and gets separated from him. The press of the crowd prevents her from boarding the train, and none of her family can get off to assist her. She is run over by the crowd, and as the train shunts off, she loses consciousness. There is a cut to that night, when she comes to. Inert bodies are lying all over the station platform; some may be asleep, some are probably unconscious and some are surely dead.

Some individuals are wandering around, possibly looking for lost friends or relatives, and there are others looking to loot or to rape. Sakina, her clothes torn and her face and body bloodied from her ordeal, gets up in a panic and starts running. A gang of predators chase and almost catch her, when she fortuitously runs into the arms of Tara Singh, a Jat who had been a delivery truck driver at the wealthy school she had attended in Shimla. The whole scene at the station had been grimly realistic until now, but the chillingly bestial ravishers now suddenly become ludicrously helpless before the prodigious strength and miraculous martial skills of Tara Singh.

Having warded off the predators at the station, Tara Singh also has to deal with the Jat Sikh population of his neighbourhood the next morning. Word has got out that he has a Muslim woman staying in his house; the neighbours, flushed with hatred for Muslims and burning with vengeance, want the girl to be handed over to them or at least have her sent to a Muslim refugee camp. So Tara Singh's epic skills have to be employed once again and, without any weapons save a lathi, he proceeds to subdue what seems like the entire male population of the town. Sakina is given no reason to doubt in any way the genuineness of Tara Singh's resolve in protecting her, for it is evident that he will go to any length to keep her from harm.

They hear a report that the train on which Sakina's family were travelling to Lahore was attacked by murderous thugs and that there were no survivors. Tara Singh takes her in his truck to the station where the train with the massacred passengers had been terminated, and amongst the dead people's belongings kept at the station, Sakina finds her father's musical pocket watch,[2] which is proof to her of the veracity of the report that there were no survivors.

Tara Singh's own parents were also killed in the riots, but his perceived need to protect the girl he had secretly loved for some years helped him to overcome any feelings of vengeance he might have once had. Of course, their relationship would seem to be infinitely more difficult than that of Romeo and Juliet, for he is a Jat Sikh and she is a Muslim; he is a lowly truck driver and she comes from a fabulously wealthy family. Community and class have placed seemingly impenetrable barriers to any relationship they might forge. Tara Singh has accepted this from the start, and when Sakina decides it would be best for all concerned if she went to the refugee camp to enable her to be sent to her uncle's house in Lahore, he resignedly agrees, but fearing her discomfort in the camp he resolves to take her to Lahore himself. Before they leave, she discovers a notebook he has kept which contains a photograph of her as well as some lines of romantic poetry he has written about her. This changes her perspective. Her new emotional state makes the trip to Lahore more difficult, but it is made a little easier for the audience by an extended song sequence in which the camera offers various versions of the end of the journey, intending, it would seem, to establish Sakina's confusion and uncertainty. When the song ends and the truck approaches the border, she slams her foot on the brake, says she will not go to Lahore, and declares her willingness to be his wife. We might underline at this point that this inter-communal relationship consists of two people, albeit socially at odds, who had known each other previously; moreover, he had given her unqualified protection when she was in dire peril. Thus their marriage is credible and respectable, and not an imposition by an abductor on a helpless woman.

Another song plays as we see their affection grow more erotic. Sakina blends in with the community now, and is soon pregnant, later giving birth to a boy. Thus, their marriage is seen to be a happy one. Then Sakina sees a stray sheet of newspaper containing a photograph of her father. From the Pakistan embassy in New Delhi, she speaks to her mother on the phone and learns that her parents had escaped the massacre on the train and that her father was now the mayor of Lahore. From the shots we see of their house there, it is evident that Ashraf Ali is a man of power and opulence.

Through the character of Ashraf Ali the film now proceeds to indulge in the assertion of a somewhat cheap binary: the demonising of Pakistan and, to a lesser extent, the lionising of India. In addition to being powerful and wealthy, Ashraf Ali is preoccupied with self-interest, making him a simple antagonist to Tara Singh. He is chauvinistically patriotic to Pakistan, voicing categorically and a number of times his intense antipathy towards India. And so, when he sends a private light aircraft to take Sakina, her husband and their son to Pakistan, and we learn that there has been a failure in properly processing the little boy's visa, we might smell a rat. Sakina does not, however, and she goes with great excitement to see her parents, whom she had given up for dead, though she is desperately tearful at having to leave behind her husband and son.

We have seen Fate play a cruel trick on Sakina, causing her to stumble just a few metres short of boarding the train. Then Fortune looked after her in leading her to Tara Singh when she was being pursued by rapists. Now Reality forces her to see her father in his true light, a man who will stop at nothing to enhance what he sees as his family's honour, even if that means the virtual destruction of his daughter's marriage and her family life. Sakina learns that it was his guile that caused the visa hitch and soon she comes to realise that he has no interest in a Jat son-in-law or a half-Jat grandson. Moreover, he insists that Sakina stay permanently in Pakistan and directs the Pakistan embassy in Delhi to keep Tara Singh and his son out of his adopted country.

Ashraf Ali does indeed maintain a manic anti-India predisposition that is innate to his fierce patriotism for Pakistan, and this most glaringly colours his role in the film. Consequently, through his particular functioning in the narrative, his prominent screen presence and specific dialogues, Ashraf Ali comes across as a tool to demonise India, and *Gadar* becomes more of a nationalist statement that overshadows the human narrative of separation and loss and whatever the eventual counterpart will be. Without having met Tara Singh, Ashraf Ali refers to him as 'the enemy'. When Tara Singh agrees to compromise his own culture for the greater happiness of his wife and son, Ashraf Ali insists not only that he accept Islam but that he publicly shout his veneration of Pakistan and cry out curses on India. At this point it all starts to get a little silly, even before the orgy of epic violence which defines the last half hour or so of the film.

Ashraf Ali is obliged to acknowledge his sins after Sakina is accidentally shot by him. With Sakina recovering in hospital, repentance comes a little too readily, but credibility confronts another challenge with the mad Kareem trumpeting Gandhi's non-violence as the only true religion. This is followed by a shot of a train, many bogeys of which had been disconnected by Tara Singh earlier in a fugitive frenzy, now whole again as a vague symbol of reunion and reconciliation.

Partition

A far more credible and commendable film on a very similar theme is *Partition* (2007) directed by Vic Sarin. The film has one notable shortcoming, at least for subcontinental viewers, and that is its loss of a degree of credibility due to it being made in English. However, what is especially interesting about it in the context of this particular discussion is its narrative similarity to *Gadar*. If *Gadar* were to be stripped of its songs and dances and other extraneous content, the structure and the major elements of its narrative would be remarkably similar to that of *Partition*.

Central to the opening section of the film are two Sikh men, Avtar and Gyan, who are soldiers in the British Indian Army and who come from the same village in the Punjab. The central strand of the narrative starts with an extraordinarily vicious act of vengeance by a group of Sikh villagers led by Avtar on a large group of Muslim refugees headed on foot for Pakistan. Those who manage to escape the slaughter flee to their destination, presumably, except for a girl, Naseem, who in the turmoil gets separated from her family. Later, well after dark, she is discovered by Gyan, alone and terrified, and he takes her to his home in the village where he gives her shelter and protection. As in most villages in the Punjab, anti-Other hostility is acute and sustained, and Naseem is rightly terrified, even to the point of wanting Gyan to shoot her so that she might attain peace. Gyan is adamant in his resolve to keep her safe. However, while he is working in the fields, her presence in his house is confirmed by a man who raises an alarm, bringing a crowd of people bent on revenge, demanding that the girl be handed over. Gyan manages to get back in time and opens the door himself to the villagers, declaring that the girl has done no wrong and that he will not allow any harm to come to her. Avtar is especially insistent that she be handed over to them, but Gyan quietly dares his comrade to kill him or be killed by him, and is grimly persuasive. The other villagers, aggressive and resentful, are assuaged by Gyan's generous gift of money to those who have suffered losses. It is all quite different, and all the more chilling, from the bellicosity with which Tara Singh deals with the predators at the station and his neighbours the next morning. After the slaughter of the refugees, this film offers very little violence, but what little there is has been made all the more horrible by its realism and intensified by its brevity.

At Naseem's request, Gyan makes an effort to take her back to the other refugees, but he is unable to trace the route they have taken, and so Naseem has no choice but to remain with him. Her hope lies in his undertaking to go to Delhi to seek the help of Margaret Stillwell, the sister of his late commanding officer in the war. Margaret agrees to take on the seemingly impossible task of trying to track down Naseem's family in Lahore, and Naseem waits, living in fear and disquieting uncertainty. In time her courage grows, while most of the other villagers, including Gyan's mother, come to realise that she is no monster but a simple, harmless girl. She insists on going out of the house to fetch water from the well, and meets with hostility from Gyan's mother's friend, Rani (against whom the mother defends

Naseem) and even makes a friend, Manjula. We see Naseem bringing Gyan his lunch in the mustard field, along with other brief and simple indications of a happiness and good humour developing between them.

A major turning point in the depiction of the growth of love between Naseem and Gyan is the celebration of the Holi festival. Naseem is pictured enjoying the unrestrained joy of it all with Manjula, her face covered with festive red *gulaal* powder. Left momentarily alone, she is grabbed and molested by the man who had earlier confirmed her presence in Gyan's house to the villagers. Gyan chances upon this and attacks the man in rage, almost strangling him, but is stopped by a quiet and understanding Avtar. The effect of all of this on Naseem is handled with cinematic brilliance and amazing economy. Naseem washes the Holi powder from her face, and that night dreams of doing the same thing, the blobs of red in the basin now being blood. She might have overcome her fear of being in a Sikh village, but she cannot rid herself of the horror of that dire attack. She wakes up, distressed, and Gyan comes to comfort her. He then starts to return to his own bed but is restrained by her hand which will not release his, and he sits on the bed beside her. Next morning he wakes to see her dancing outside in the rain, a smile on her face. It is a tellingly artistic version of Sakina's discovery of Tara Singh's notebooks, and a clear indication of the direction the narrative will now take.

In time they are married according to the Sikh tradition and then we see them playing with their little boy. This concertina technique of presenting in a very short sequence the major events of a much longer period of time is very similar to the one employed in *Gadar*. It is clear that they are truly in love, and in playing with the little boy on the swing and teaching him to fly a kite they appear to be a very happy family. Then, quite out of the blue, Margaret Stillwell turns up at their house.

Just as Sakina had fortuitously come upon a stray sheet of newspaper bearing her father's photograph, Margaret, through the more mundane workings of the ministry for the reunification of families, has managed to track down Naseem's family in Lahore. She even has the address and travel papers for Naseem. Gyan cannot go with her, as at that time of international tension only Muslims could go to Pakistan. So she sets out on her own, with a return bus ticket that will bring her back in one month, but when Gyan and the little boy, Vijay, go to meet her on her return, she is not on the bus.

We see Naseem being welcomed emotionally by her brothers, Akbar and Zakir, and her mother, but she is sad to learn that her father 'didn't survive the massacre. He was killed by the Sikhs the day we lost you.' The sustained animosity cannot be missed. Indeed, it soon transpires that Naseem, like Sakina, has been imprisoned in her family's home in Pakistan and her brothers and mother insist that she stay there. Her letters to Gyan have not been sent and his have been hidden from her. She tries to leave but Akbar locks her in her room.

Like Tara Singh, who cannot get the papers to travel to Pakistan, Gyan decides to cross the border illegally and on foot. Believing Margaret Stillwell's assurance that if he were Muslim he could walk into Pakistan, he adopts a Muslim name and appearance, discarding his turban for a Muslim prayer cap and having his hair cut and his beard trimmed. However, he is turned back by Border Control for not having adequate documentation. That night he and Vijay crawl under the wire and head towards Lahore.

Tara Singh's entry to his father-in-law's house is extravagant in the extreme. Gyan, on the other hand, has the gate opened for him by Akbar and almost immediately Naseem, having recognised him from the window, runs to him, but they are forcibly separated by the two brothers. Naseem is dragged inside and Gyan is brutally beaten and kicked by Akbar. He does not try to retaliate; perhaps he sees no point. He simply says, 'I was a soldier. I killed many men. I came home looking for peace. I found Partition and hate everywhere. I wanted no part of it.' He is taken to Lahore, where Margaret acts on his behalf. Naseem's mother eventually relents and helps her daughter get out of the house and she meets up with Gyan at the railway station where Margaret has managed to take him and Vijay.

The ending is horrifically credible, though nothing like the 20-minute spectacular ending of *Gadar*. Gyan, and Naseem and Vijay almost make it to the train together, but they are pursued by Akbar and Zakir. Akbar and Gyan are locked in a struggle on the high footbridge joining the platforms, and while Naseem joins her son and Margaret by the train, Gyan is flung to his death onto the tracks below. It is utterly plausible, ghastly and consonant with the brutal emotions of the time.

There is an ending after the ending, which perhaps makes it anticlimactic, compromising the horror—so characteristic of the Partition—of the scene at the railway station. Naseem has gone to England with Margaret. She tells us, 'Gyan's love gave me the strength to start a new life. He lives on in all that I am, all that we are.' There is an echo in this of Gyan's plea to Akbar: 'I had to save Naseem, but it was Naseem who saved me. Your sister gave me back my life.' Yet the reality is familial destruction, an all too frequent reality of the Partition, which had sundered a family of three good people.

Pinjar

Gadar and *Partition* tell the stories of cross-communal couples brought together by the woman's need for protection. Each couple has its unity threatened and subjected to stress; one couple survives the challenge, the other succumbs to hate-inspired, mindless violence. Chandra Prakash Dwivedi's *Pinjar* ('Beyond Boundaries', 2003) presents the extraordinary story of a young Hindu woman abducted by a Muslim man, kept prisoner for some time and then forcibly married to him, so setting up an ending that is controversial. *Pinjar* is another long and sometimes cluttered film of more than three hours, in which form is occasionally compromised by indulgence in a song or secondary element of narrative; nevertheless, the film is saved by a defining care for its focal narrative.

The abduction of the Hindu girl, Puro, by the young Muslim man, Rashid, is not an act of communal spite fired by the upheaval of irrationality brought about by the Partition. Rather, the hostile mood of the time is exploited by an acrimonious uncle of Rashid, whose family has been for generations in disputation of one kind or another with Puro's, mostly over matters of property. The uncle sees an opportunity, given the weight of numbers and the prevailing climate of antagonism, to strike a telling advantage over his rival in this petty feud between the Sheiks and the Sahas. Moreover, Rashid is besotted by Puro, despite having first met her in an amusing accident in which he might have been somewhat humiliated.

As is the case in *Chhalia*, notions of Hindu honour and respectability override any serious intent to rescue the girl. She has become polluted and no one will ever want to marry her. Who then would look after her? She would be an indelible and constant cause of disgrace to her parents, and a curse to the marriage prospects of her siblings. Thus, it is not difficult for the abduction to become a prolonged imprisonment. At one point, Puro is able to get away from Rashid and throws herself at the mercy of her parents; however, there is no mercy to be had from them and she is cruelly and unambiguously rejected. Rashid is waiting for her outside and his compassionate reception of her is particularly significant. There is no punishment or even admonishment for her attempted escape; rather, he welcomes her back tenderly and, at least for a moment, his gentleness stands in stark contrast to the callous and craven righteousness of her parents.

While there is no obvious link between the abduction and the Partition, there is indeed a very clear analogous connection. We learn from Rashid that this inter-familial conflict has gone on for generations and that the enmity is based on some property swindle, exacerbated by communal differences that gave rise to a string of tit-for-tat reprisals, just as so much Partition violence was little more than righteous retaliation. In Puro's case, this *lex talionis* was a fearsome principle as it meant that her parents' intense fear that the Sheiks might kill them was fundamental to their rejection of their daughter. Yet the law of righteous retaliation allows for no reasonable answer to Puro's perfectly reasonable question: 'My uncle kidnapped your aunt, but where is my fault in that?' The unexpected twist in this unusual tale is the fact that Rashid appreciates the reasoning in Puro's question, and given that it is now too late for her parents to even consider taking her back, he replaces the love lost from them with a tenderness of his own.

Their marriage is really a formalising of what their relationship has become, and given the conventional societal view of her as polluted, her options beyond Rashid are virtually nil. He gives Puro the Muslim name of Hamida and has it tattooed on the inside of her forearm—something that causes her obvious distress—as though it has erased all traces of her previous life as it will not be washed off in the future. Ironically, though, the tattoo will save her life later in the film.

As the broader society becomes more restive, their marriage seems to become less uncertain. However, Rashid decides that they will move to another village as Hindus may hear about their marriage and cause trouble. Then there is talk among young Congress workers of concerns about the simmering Hindu–Muslim violence, and at a Congress rally an impassioned speech against the notion of partition is delivered. In a secondary plot development, an interesting emblem of communalism is presented. A mentally deranged girl from the neighbourhood gives birth in the fields. Puro, followed by Rashid, rushes to help her; they are able to save the baby, but the girl dies. Prior to this, Puro's own baby was stillborn and she takes the mad girl's baby as though it is a godsend. However, six months after the birth, the baby gives rise to contention as the village elders claim that the child is a Hindu and should be brought up by Hindus, despite no one knowing who the father was, let alone his communal identity. It seems that the intention is to deprive the Muslim couple of their baby rather than to provide an appropriate upbringing for the child. Rashid is summoned by them and their views are made clear in language that is clearly menacing. He is ordered, threateningly, to surrender the infant to them. A little later the baby is wrested from Puro and she wonders who else is left for her to lose. In fact, Puro will soon become an agent of reconciliation rather than a victim of further loss.

In an extraordinary act of spite, Puro's brother, Trilok, sets fire to the soon-to-be-harvested fields owned by Rashid's family. They lose everything. When Rashid shares his suspicion of Trilok with Puro, she senses his hurt and, in a curious way, feels pity for Rashid. Just as curiously, Rashid expresses an unusual degree of understanding for Trilok. 'His heart must be full of love and pain for you,' he tells her. The potential for storminess in the marriage seems to have dwindled greatly, especially as Puro appears to have come to accept that any flicker of hope in her restoration to her earlier life would be utterly fruitless.

There is a title card indicating that a year has passed. It is 1947 and carloads of vociferous, flag-waving supporters are seen. The Partition has been enacted and another communal riot is about to start. Rashid and Puro are in what has become Pakistan and do not have to join the migratory columns of hordes of refugees. They are fortunate, as is made clear with some scenes of terrible rioting and the vicious slaughter of those trying to leave.

Circumstances conspire—conveniently perhaps but not altogether incredibly—to bring remnants of Puro's earlier life together. Ramchand, the man to whom she was all too briefly betrothed, meets her by chance; he connects with Puro's brother, Trilok; and Rashid and Puro cooperate resolutely in rescuing Ramchand's sister, Lajo, from her more common state of abduction by a Muslim man. There is the reunion of Ramchand and Trilok in Lahore where Rashid brings Puro and Lajo. Puro's meeting with her beloved brother again is intensely emotional. Then, as they move towards the truck that will take them to Amritsar and safety in India, Rashid silently fades out of the picture, resigned to what he might have thought was inevitable. Unexpectedly, however, his wife spends some anxious minutes in finding him before saying goodbye to Trilok, Ramchand and Lajo, and then returning home with her husband.

The turmoil that was the Partition of India did not often allow for moral absolutes. Notions of right and wrong were usually conditional, requiring modifiers such as *up to a point*, *by and large*, *under the circumstances*, or *in the long run* to qualify them. It might be said that Puro's decision was not entirely right, given that it exonerated abduction, false imprisonment and forced marriage. No doubt the first of these, the abduction, cannot be whitewashed; a civilised society does not allow for the theft of material things let alone people. However, Rashid never tries to exculpate himself of his regrettable action, explaining it—rather than justifying it—on what he cites as two grounds: the pressure of his family and his love for Puro. As far as Dwivedi's film is concerned, the latter is of greater interest, and so most of the film shows us a remorseful Rashid, yet one unable to fully expiate his sin; when he comes close to expiation, Puro obviates its necessity.

The actual physical touch of Rashid in the act of sweeping Puro off her feet and onto his horse would be enough in orthodox Hindu eyes to disqualify her from her impending marriage. Rashid might have thought to return her to her parents, but her parents' distress about their threatened social status could be assuaged only by considering her dead. Towards the end of the film we are given a glimpse of the Muslim abductor of Lajo, and it is easy to guess that he is a self-interested, self-indulgent, authoritarian boor; by no means is Rashid to be compared with him. There is no evidence of bullying on Rashid's part, nor of neglect or abuse. He cares not only for Puro, but for what Puro cares for; he tries to save the mad girl during childbirth and he allows for her child to be cared for in his house by Puro for six months; he engages with the rescue of Lajo, playing an important part in it and in her continuing protection; and he personally conveys Puro and Lajo to Lahore whence they may proceed to safety in India. This last act is, perhaps, his real effort at expiation. To throw ethics into confusion, Puro no longer needs his expiation; accepting her parents' rejection she is now able to accept the abduction, and she comes to see that Rashid's love for her is undeniably genuine. It is an extraordinary ending, and a very moving one.

Khamosh Pani

The Pakistani film, *Khamosh Pani* ('Silent Waters', 2003), made by Sabiha Sumar based on her own short story considers the experience of arbitrary dislocation well after the event. Here it is not so much the experience of displacement that comes into focus but its ramifications years later. In this case the displaced victim, as in most cases a woman, is not abducted but given refuge by those who might have been thought to abduct and misuse her. The narrative germinates in a situation similar to the beginning of the focal relationship in *Partition,* but what makes this story different is the fact that the woman is desperate to escape the clutches of two sets of predators: her own people and those of the Other.

Khamosh Pani is set in Pakistan in 1979, soon after the assumption of the Presidency of the country by General Zia-ul-Haq, remembered for his re-imposition of martial law, his hanging of his elected predecessor, Zulfikar Ali Bhutto, and his endeavours to Islamise the state of Pakistan. Central to the narrative is Ayesha, the widowed mother of Salim, a young man approaching adulthood, but her story is inextricably linked to what happened in 1947, a time that does not seem to be as directly relevant to the lives of Ayesha's friends and family as it is to her. Consequently, the suggestive or undeveloped flashbacks to 1947 are perceived as pertaining exclusively to Ayesha and bearing even an arcane and ineradicable significance to her life. The exclusivity of the flashback sequences is underlined by their being in black and white, the fact that they are generally devoid of faces, and their central visual allusion to a well.

Ayesha's life underwent a profound change at the time of her flight across the new border. Some 30 years or so after the Partition it would seem that she has absorbed that change and managed to make of it a simple and happy life. However, her contentment, as the narrative of the film intends to show, would be tragically compromised by bigotry. Her original crisis was thrown up by the moral chaos that prospered in the acrimonious bigotry innate to Partition; her second and final crisis is prompted by a revised, chauvinistic version of that, incidentally conditioned by a gauche and insensitive endeavour to redirect a very minor by-lane of history. The first turning point is treated by the flashback sequences; the second is integral to the film's core narrative. The black-and-white and somewhat distorted vision of the former contrasts significantly with the colour and realism of the latter, suggesting—at least on the surface—two different worlds, yet the denouement of the film assures us that a lot does really stay the same.

We learn from a young girl that Ayesha never goes to the well but enjoys the favours of others bringing water for her. This introduces the first flashback sequence. There is a cut to a black-and-white shot of children running around a well and heard over is Ayesha's voice, 'We used to run around a lot. How could we know that we would keep on running?' On another occasion, while spreading out chillies to dry in the sun, Shanno asks Ayesha if she ever remembers her husband, who apparently died when their son, Salim, was very young. Here, there is another black-and-white shot of a well and Ayesha's voice-over suggests her having once belonged to the Sikh community. She mentions the birth of two nations and how men would take others' wives and some would take a knife to their own daughters. Now it is clear that the well is the symbol of Sikh female suicide, committed in order to preserve the honour of the community, and the mention of knives is a reference to fathers, husbands and brothers who killed their own women for the sake of the same perceived honour.

Here and there as the film proceeds we are given some brief flashbacks to the motif of the well, which would seem to be an indelible memory in Ayesha's mind. There is a shot of the surface of the water at the bottom of the well as though seen by Ayesha looking down on it. Later there is a shot of a young woman running away from the well and being caught by a group of men. Then there is a shot of the fugitive woman being defended against a would-be abuser. Eventually we come to the flashback that reveals the point of the well in this woman's traumatic memory. The shot is of women jumping, one after another, to their deaths in order to save their honour. A girl screams out her unwillingness to join them and there is a shot of her running away with cries for her to stay. The girl is shown running, then held up by two men who take her away. A little later we see another black-and-white flashback of the girl being fed by one of the men; she lays her head on his shoulder. He treats her with evident tenderness and tells her that he will marry her.

So cinema tells us the story of yet another woman who finds refuge in the arms of a man of a hostile community. While historians and sociologists give us substantial evidence of most cross-communal Partition marriages being subsequent to abduction, though usually without the genuine love that characterises the extraordinarily unconventional relationship in *Pinjar,* for example, it is not entirely unrealistic to imagine that happiness of a sort could have emanated out of the particular horrors that were innate to the Partition. However, *Khamosh Pani* is not about the marriage of Ayesha and the man who saved her. Much that is pertinent to the reality of Ayesha in the time in which the film is set is presented in the brief black-and-white flashbacks or is easily inferred from the core narrative, where Ayesha is presented as a conventional and devout Muslim woman. We see her at prayer and we see her giving religious instruction to a small class of little girls in the courtyard of her home. There is no reason to assume that her acceptance of Islam was in any way forcibly imposed on her. Fundamental to her faith is her own commitment to it.

It is towards the end of the film where the core narrative picks up from the flashbacks. We are told that the president of the time, the orthodox General Zia-ul-Haq, has granted permission to Sikh pilgrims from India to visit Sikh shrines in Pakistan. A very large number of Sikhs come to visit the small town in which Ayesha and Salim live and it transpires that one of them is Jaswant, younger brother of Ayesha who was known to her own family as Veero. He carries with him a locket containing a picture of her all those years earlier, a locket that was thrust into his hand when she made her desperate escape from the paternally-decreed suicide. He finds her and is not happily received by her. He pleads with her that their father is dying and would like to see her. Her reply is biting but not unjustified: 'Why? To complete what he didn't finish last time?' We have here a very blatant inversion of the 'death before dishonour' ethic so readily lauded in Indian tradition. Ayesha asserts that it was for his own peace that he wanted her dead some 30 years earlier. She also questions his good faith in accepting her alive and as a Muslim.

It is easy to sympathise with Ayesha's view of what she has been through, but it is very difficult to accept the hostility of her son, Salim, at the fact that his mother was born an infidel. A major element in the core narrative is the religious radicalisation of Salim, and that will be treated in a later chapter. At this stage let us recognise that given the kind of indoctrination he has undergone, his loving and devoted mother has sadly become devalued in his eyes. It is this, and not the twisted notion of a woman's honour fanatically upheld by men, that leads her to the well that she has always been unwilling to visit and to unhesitatingly jump in.

Khamosh Pani tells the story of a woman who was fortunate enough to salvage some happiness out of her personal nightmare of Partition. It also presents us with the bitter irony of that simple happiness being destroyed by the zealots who relentlessly demanded the partition in the first place, and their heirs who took that chauvinism some way forward in the time of Zia-ul-Haq.

The films discussed so far in this chapter make it clear that among émigré people the Partition was particularly perilous for women. As long as a woman had a husband or father to look after her, her risks were minimised, but if she ever got separated from her male guardian she might become critically vulnerable to abduction or rape, usually followed by desertion and further trauma or even murder or suicide. Given the good offices of government and non-government organisations, many of the abductions were resolved by the woman being repatriated to her family, though sadly this did not always mean that she was accepted by them. Puro's parents in *Pinjar* are a clear example of socio-religious conventions overriding familial ties, in stubbornly upholding a cruel unconcern even for their own innocent daughter's suffering. There were indeed men like Tara Singh in *Gadar*, Gyan in *Partition*, Rashid in *Pinjar* and, apparently, Salim's father in *Khamosh Pani* who were decent, humane, chivalrous, courageous, even heroic; unfortunately, not all separated and displaced women had the good luck to fall into the arms of such men.

Viceroy's House revisited

We might now take up the story of Aalia and Jeet, from *Viceroy's House*, whom we met in Chapter 1. Their love story was threatened by its own partition with the return from England of Asif, the man who had been chosen *for* Aalia though not *by* her. Now that private partition is exacerbated by the vast maelstrom in which millions of others have been caught. Cowed by the escalating violence and no longer enjoying the security of the Viceroy's House, for the riot had reached even there, Aalia resolves to take her blind elderly father to Lahore, where she will stay in Asif's house until he joins them at a later date. The last time Jeet sees her is when she is driven away to take the train to Lahore. On one level it might seem as though it is Asif who has taken her out of his life, but the political overtones are unmistakeable: quite clearly the Partition is furthering its work of alienating simple, powerless people from one another and their homes.

The social ramifications of the great division were too complex and too dire for there to be a simple end to it. Quite credibly—and horribly so—Jeet reads in the newspaper that the train in which Aalia and her father were travelling had been attacked and there were no survivors. It was in the nature of the way in which Pakistan was born that obviated any certainty in the idea of simply opting for one side of the new border, going there and starting a new life. The reality of dislocation and migration was fraught with hardship, usually dangerous and often horrific. And given the constant likelihood of the ghoulish unexpected, the experience was beset by many elements more likely to pertain to Hindi cinema, though very often the realities in which people found themselves entangled were even more bizarre than all the fictions of Bollywood.

In a sense the newspaper report is true in stating that there were no survivors of the attack on the train; at least no survivors could be found when rescuers reached the scene of the slaughter. Aalia, however, did survive, thanks to her father's fear for her honour. Just like the many husbands and fathers who aided their wives in jumping into wells or in allowing themselves to be butchered in order to avoid the horror of rape, so did Aalia's father push her off the train to avoid the shame of what the marauders might do to her. She survived the fall and was eventually picked up by an elderly woman whose own daughter had been abducted from her; Aalia was looked after maternally by her and brought to the refugee camp in Delhi, where Jeet was trying to overcome tragedy by immersing himself in humanitarian work. Happily they find each other, as very many others did, and many thousands of others did not.

Bajrangi Bhaijaan

In his documentary on the eastern partition, *Simantarekha,* Tanvir Mokammel muses on the rigidity of borders in South Asia in comparison with the fluidity of national boundaries between countries in western Europe that might once have been described as long-time traditional enemies. Yet, in the maintenance of border infrangibility by Pakistani, Bangladeshi and Indian forces, there is a suggestion that vigilance is necessary to maintain hostility, and that enmity is not innate to subcontinental nationalism but has to be nurtured. Violating the border, particularly in the west, attracts extremely severe punishment, as though being out of place without the appropriate pieces of paper is tantamount to threatening the security of an entire nation. There are two films we might look at that suggest that even children can be seen as potential threats to a nation's security.

In Kabir Khan's *Bajrangi Bhaijaan* ('Brother Bajrangi', 2015) the focus is on a heart-stealing little Pakistani girl, Shahida, who was made mute by the trauma of a frightening accident. Nationalism is established naturally and simply through a scene in which a number of jubilant rustic folk are watching a telecast of a One Day International (ODI) cricket match in which Pakistan defeats India. While nationalism or even patriotism might be significant here, cricket can never be likened to armed warfare, for true cricket enthusiasts will always transcend defeat to relish the virtues of a game played well. Though an international contest involves 'Us' and 'Them', cricket is, ironically, much more of a unifying force than a stimulus to hostility. This film will show national distinctions to be largely contrived and of little consequence, especially when they emerge as threats to basic humanity.

The little girl's mother accepts the advice to take Shahida to the *dargah* or mausoleum of a Sufi saint in a faith-based bid to regain her powers of speech. In a significant reminder that the two countries were once one, mother and daughter take the train to Delhi, where the dargah of Hazrat Nizamuddin Auliya is situated. On the way back, while the train is still in India, Shahida becomes separated from both her mother and the train in a credible series of innocent actions, setting up the nightmarish situation that suffuses the rest of the film. The nightmare of a mute little girl in a foreign country without documents does not last long, for by chance Shahida meets Pawan Kumar Chaturvedi, a Brahman, known by his nickname 'Bajrangi' because of his profound devotion to Bajrang Bali or Lord Hanuman, the monkey hero of the *Ramayana*. We meet Pawan, good for nothing other than wrestling as it transpires, in a spectacular mass song and dance sequence celebrating Bajrang Bali, a sequence that also establishes beyond any doubt the commercial nature of the film. However, despite its unrestrained populism, the film deals quite intelligently with the notion of religious difference. Shahida cannot tell Pawan even her name, and so he calls her Munni, simply assuming from her fair complexion and light hair that she is a Brahman girl, but then quite unwittingly certain actions reveal her to be a Muslim with her home and family in Pakistan. Entwined with this narrative strand is the story of Pawan's love for Rasika, in whose father's house he and Munni stay. It is a rigidly orthodox Brahman household. In time the facts of religious difference are revealed while Shahida, or Munni, gradually becomes embedded in the hearts of Pawan and Rasika. The second half of the film deals with the long, arduous and at times painful journey of Pawan and Munni to and through Pakistan to find the little girl's home. The film does, naturally, have a happy ending, as Munni's home is found (again, the process is quite credible), she regains her power of speech, and Pawan will, one can be sure, marry Rasika.

Perhaps the film betrays a degree of one-upmanship in its moralism, giving the moral high ground to India and to Hinduism in that Bajrang Bali would seem to be the ultimate victor, bearing Pawan through his gruelling ordeal wherein he single-handedly fights the Pakistan border patrol and sections of the Pakistan police, notable in the film for their blatant stupidity as well as their savage brutality. However, the appeal through the viral potentialities of the internet by the Pakistani journalist, Nawab Chand, stresses the importance of humanitarian values overriding religious differences and we see a mass response to the appeal from both the western and eastern sides of the border. The response, albeit highly improbable, is an earnest celebration of the values that would transcend the notion of the rigid distinctness of nation-states and the borders that would make them impermeable and protect their identities. While Shahida's being mute gives an interesting narrative inflection to *Bajrangi Bhaijaan*, symbolically it serves to strip her of personality and reduce her to sheer personhood, just as the two men in *Kya Dilli Kya Lahore* are reduced to being simply men after the removal of manufactured values and contrived attitudes. Thus, it is pure humanity that stands up to the challenges of moribund tradition in India and on whose behalf people readily act in Pakistan.

Ramchand Pakistani

A somewhat worthier work with a similar narrative nucleus is a Pakistani film, Mehreen Jabbar's *Ramchand Pakistani* (2008). This film is set decades after the Partition, but its significance to this discourse is in the persistence of the mutual hostility that to some extent generated the Partition and continues even today. Tensions between India and Pakistan at the turn of the present century and after had existed in 1947, although certain instrumentalities of tension, such as terrorist organisations, were later developments. Nevertheless, the national paranoia that colours the fraught relations between India and Pakistan today is very much a product of the kind of thinking that engendered the Two Nation Theory or, at least, were assumed by it.

Much of the Radcliffe Line in the east is marked by a barbed wire fence. This is also the case in the west, but there are stretches of it that are not marked clearly, but are marked by white painted rocks on the ground, their actual significance being not at all obvious, especially to adventurous little boys. *Ramchand Pakistani* is not about the Partition as such but about a severe and brutal ramification brought about by the fateful line that the Partition necessitated.

Ramchand is the little boy of a Dalit (Untouchable) family in Pakistan. The opening scenes of the film focus on the nine-year-old, readily lovable and mercurially naughty. Having run from one of his many delinquencies and become absorbed with notions of the injustice of his world, he unwittingly strays between the white painted rocks and into India. He is almost immediately picked up by two soldiers of an Indian border patrol who cannot seem to suspect that a nine-year-old boy armed with a slingshot is unlikely to be a threat to the world's largest democracy and a nuclear power. A little later, his father—a simple farmer and primary school teacher—comes looking for him, and walks into a similar trap. The only good to come of this absurd situation is that the two of them are imprisoned together. The mentality that cannot rule out the suspicion of terrorism in a young boy and his humble unarmed father gives rise to a situation that is frighteningly absurd. Though both he and Ramchand answer their questions promptly and unequivocally, making their identities clearly genuine, they are still jailed indefinitely and without trial. A pre-titles card might have put this 'absurdity' into some kind of context by pointing out that the events depicted here follow the attack on the Indian Parliament in December

2001 by agents of Lashkar-e-Taiba and Jaish-e-Mohammed, two Pakistan-based terrorist organisations, hence putting border patrols on both sides of the line on extraordinarily high alert.[3]

The absurdity plummets very quickly into brutality as we see a shot of Shankar, the father, hanging upside down from the ceiling and being beaten. He is taken down and only then is he, along with Ramchand, put to basic interrogation, in this case the provision of personal details. Their genitals have been examined and their uncircumcised condition is evidence that they are not Muslim. The simple questions regarding age, name, caste, village, education and the like are answered promptly and consistently by father and son, but it would appear simpler to incarcerate them rather than check their stories, give them both a kick in the pants, and escort them back to Pakistan. And so a humble Dalit teacher and landless farmer and his nine-year-old son begin a term of more than four years in an Indian jail. Champa, their wife and mother at home in the village, is told nothing of her family's whereabouts.

There are, one can be sure, many jails in the world much worse than the one in which Shankar and his little boy are incarcerated. Nevertheless, the jail is no place for an innocent man and certainly not for a little boy. The prison is overcrowded with men, many of them of questionable character. At night there are bronchial sounds, flatulence, men distressed by nightmares. An old man dies one night in their cell; on another occasion, there is a serious brawl. One man tries to seduce Ramchand into smoking; others are interested in him for another kind of seduction. Shankar is drawn into violence on several occasions to protect his son, as they lead a life in limbo in this hellish place. Particularly difficult for them is the oppressive uncertainty that hangs over them. They have had no trial and no sentence has been passed. They may long for release, but they have no idea when it will come—*if* it will come.

The Partition which gave rise to the white painted rocks between which Ramchand inadvertently wanders has also created other partitions, one of which divides Shankar's family. While father and son languish in dark uncertainty in an Indian prison, Champa, the wife and mother they sorely miss, continues the day-to-day struggle for existence that is life for one as humble as she. The absence of a husband makes her subject to economic exploitation and vulnerable to the unwanted advances of men.

We are also given a subtle reminder of another, age-old partition in Hinduism, that between Untouchables and the rest of society. A female police officer in the jail is assigned the task of supervising Ramchand in order to keep him, as much as possible, from the potential danger of mixing with the other prisoners, all of whom are adult. At first she sees this as an affront to her feminist dignity, but very soon she, like everyone else, becomes fond of the boy. Yet the traditional boundary is ineradicably there, as indicated by her stern insistence that he not touch her cups and plates for fear of the pollution he would surely inflict on them. Nationality carries no meaning in their relationship; caste does. But then familiarity often breeds the opposite of contempt, and having told him to ask his father to tie a new protective thread around his wrist, we see her a little later tying it herself. Then they sit down together to watch a video cassette—but not too close! Such profound social partitions might not be obviated but they can at least be diluted.

After Shankar's attack on Ramchand's predator, the father and son are brought before the superintendent. Shankar's anger has lessened his subservience and he tells the officer quite candidly that they have been brought to this prison without charge or trial and no care is given to their safety. The best the officer can do in response is to suggest that Shankar go and see 'how Pakistanis treat our prisoners in their jails'. It is a feeble argument but one which lies at the heart of the utterly unworthy human emotion of revenge, the leading villain in all communal disputation, violence, rapes and killings. The notion that 'we might be bad, but they are worse' may be true, but it does not obviate 'our' guilt.

The nightmare in which Ramchand and his father are caught is something perplexingly vague, an ensnarement without apparent form or structure and unapproachable in its anonymity. Champa tries to approach it through the local officials and is disheartened to overhear a conversation between two of them revealing that efforts on her behalf have been given up. The fact is that no one really cares about these captives, yet they are not to be freed—and for this no reason or any attempt at justification is given, simply because it does not have to be. Then suddenly the nightmare is diluted with promise, and Ramchand and Shankar are released, but some time later an unexplained clerical hitch brings them back to the jail. Eventually Ramchand is released, heartbreakingly leaving his father behind, and soon returns to a joyous reunion with his mother. A title card tells us that Shankar also returns, a little later.

It has all been a deplorable waste—a waste of prison resources and public money, and a waste of what might have been a happy family life. It has also exerted an awful psychological effect on an innocent man and his little boy. The dreadful uncertainty of being where one does not belong and not knowing when, if ever, release is to be obtained, has coloured their days and nights for around five or six years. However, it might have been so much worse were it not for what turned out to be the good fortune of Shankar being arrested too. Had Ramchand had to bear the incarceration on his own, a much more horrible story might have had to be told.

Ramchand Pakistani is a beautiful film that focuses on a hasty and ill-considered fracturing of a poor family. We might well wonder what the Partition of India in 1947 did to enhance the lives of people like Shankar, his wife and son. It is even more baffling to try to imagine how the partition of his family, without reason, trial, documentation or provision of any form of information, safeguarded the security of India. Are nine-year-old boys and their humble Dalit fathers a potential threat to national security? Here lies the absurdity that the Two Nation Theory had reduced itself to.

The material presented in this chapter offers a clear distinction between populist films and those with a more serious intent. In *Chhalia* and *Gadar*, notions of the Partition often seem to be diluted to the foreground, as appealing though less relevant narrative elements provide a platform for popular entertainment, especially in the form of spectacular physical conflict. *Gadar* is, nevertheless, one of four significant films dealing with an interesting theme that would seem to be the converse of Partition actuality. There is an immense literature documenting the widespread abuse of women that went along with the bigotries, conflicts and enactments of retribution at the time of the division of the country. To find four films in which a man finds himself in a position of power over a woman of the Other community should not be at all surprising; what is remarkable is the humanity and decency shown by those men towards their female charges. Of course, they were not typical, but our faith in humanity might be largely dependent on being able to believe that at least some men like them did indeed exist. We might also take heart from the laudability of the women, especially in *Pinjar* and *Khamosh Pani*. Four women who might have been horribly abused and worse, actually find love and devotion, one of them only to lose it, though not before it had changed her life. These women had been lost to a previous chapter in their lives and, as their respective films come to an end, we see them now enabled to write new chapters for themselves.

The two children discussed here had been lost in a real, literal sense, and are totally dependent on the good offices of others in order to be found again. While Shahida's being mute gives an interesting narrative inflection to *Bajrangi Bhaijaan*, it has the symbolic value of both essentialising and universalising the character that mobilises so many to act selflessly on her behalf.

Ramchand is caught in an even worse situation. Although he is lucky enough to have his father with him, the two of them nevertheless remain imprisoned and at the mercy of a foreign and hostile power. The apparent inanity of such excessive treatment of a once mischievous little boy and his humble father might well make us wonder what, in fact, Radcliffe's masters had bade him create all those years earlier.

Notes and References

1. 'Chhalia' is the name of the male lead.

2. When opened, the watch plays the tune of the popular American song, *Que sera*, which was made famous by Doris Day and released in 1956, nine years after the Partition!

3. Five of the terrorists were killed as were 14 Indians—police and security personnel, and a gardener.

five

The Descent into Mayhem

In the realm of fairytale history, where people might have done this instead of that and decisions were made with the benefit of foresight and tempered by notions of justice and the good of all, a partition might have been enacted the effects of which would have been no more seismic than those of a landslide general election. Actual history, however, is daubed with the mud and slush of decisions that were wrong because they were misguided, deceitful or simply perverse. The thought that a peaceful partition might have been enacted by an authoritarian, imperialist regime, obliged, by what it perceived to be its own future interests in the Indian Ocean, to pay heed to the menacing rhetoric of Jinnah and the Muslim League, and faced with the nightmare of resolving deep-rooted problems with the 'other' India—the militant Sikhs, the 60,000,000 shamefully oppressed Untouchables, and the huge majority of Hindus of a multitude of hierarchically-ordered castes, liberal and conservative, moderate and extremist—could not have been dreamt up even by a partnership of Alice and Pollyanna.

It is impossible to look at the Partition of India and not be struck by its horrendous violence, violence that was pervasive and constant, grotesque in its conception and infinite in the variety of its cruelty. The first several years of free India and newly-created Pakistan were a trough in the history of civilisation, a gruesome descent into mayhem. It was a time when violence was perpetrated without the restraint of conscience or the strategy of reason, urged on by that which is most unworthy in the human psyche: the lust for revenge coloured by misinformed beliefs about the need to defend 'our' values, 'our' tradition, 'our' forefathers' legacy and even 'our' God. Values, tradition, forefathers and God are indeed fundamental to a religiously defined community, and communalism was fundamental to the scourge of violence unleashed by the Partition.

However, communal violence was not engendered by the enactment of Partition, but had been simmering in one way or another, here and there, for many years. Long before the division of the country had been mooted, there had been occasional expressions of public unrest. For example, the riots in Bengal from the early years of the twentieth century had at least some connection with the deliberate noise pollution outside places of worship or the slaughter of cows or pigs with the intention to make mischief, but there were often socio-economic factors more prominently involved. Moreover, after the enthusiasm of the Non-Cooperation Movement of the early 1920s started to die down, the zeal for Hindu–Muslim unity dwindled too, for various reasons, but mainly due to the natural death of the circumstantially doomed Khilafat Movement. Later, communal suspicion and mistrust grew in the years after the Lahore Resolution and it spurred on local, sporadic riots that swelled to an unprecedented level of barbarity in the Calcutta Killings emanating out of Jinnah's Direct Action Day of 16 August 1946, a year before the Partition. Yet even the horrors of the Calcutta Killings were surpassed in savagery when the Punjab and Bengal were plunged into hellishness by the stroke of Radcliffe's pencil.

The last year or so of British rule in India was abjectly mishandled. Excitement at India's imminent independence was tempered by uncertainty about the future territorial integrity of the country. While there was a vociferous demand for partition, particularly from one quarter, in order to allow for the creation of Pakistan, there were calls just as strident to avert it at any cost. Whereas there was a strong suspicion that a partition might be enacted, there was no certainty concerning where the lines would be drawn. Particularly in the northwest and in Bengal, millions were beset with the worry of not knowing whether they would remain Indians or would find themselves living in Pakistan. Along with suspicion, rumours were rife and, as is so often the case with hearsay, the rumours fertilised the ground for mistrust, hatred and violence. As people were deliberately kept in the dark, ignorance ruled, making this fertilisation all the more effective. When one stood to lose everything one possessed, including one's links with the past, the intensity of fear and worry was understandable.

Tamas

Govind Nihalani's epic, *Tamas* ('Darkness', 1987) is one of the most valuable contributions to Partition cinema. Based on the novel of the same name by Bhisham Sahni, it was originally intended to be shown as a feature film despite its extraordinary running time of just under five hours, but after threats by Hindu extremists and court action it was resolved that it should be presented episodically, as a television series, presumably to obviate public disorder from the likely picketing and vandalising of cinema halls.

Fundamental to separatist thinking are the notions of disputation and conflict, the intensity of which is such that social harmony and tranquillity would seem to be unattainable and so, early in the film, the particular interest groups are established—the Congress Party, the Muslim League, the Hindu Mahasabha and the British administration—though the emanations of disputation and conflict emerge only gradually. At first there is little, if anything, more than the rivalry akin to that between ambitious sports teams. A small group of Congress leaders takes to the streets singing patriotic songs and raising slogans; they confront a similarly small group representing the Muslim League doing much the same thing, though seemingly with a little more passion and just a hint of malice. Their leader accuses the Congress of being a Hindu party and dismisses the notion of Indian independence as being really Hindu independence, while the argument that the Congress includes Indians of all communities, including Muslims, is met with derision. Nevertheless, civility, though evidently strained, tempers this contention.

It is when the Congress group, in accordance with Gandhian social discipline, go to clean sewage drains and gutters—choosing a little unwisely, perhaps, a Muslim locality in which to humble themselves in the interests of the greater good—that there is a hint that something is amiss and danger may be imminent. A group of men arrive and give instructions to all in the lane to go inside quickly and stay hidden. It is only here that we learn the full significance of the extraordinary opening scene of the film.

The film opens with an Untouchable, Nathu, being commissioned to kill a pig for someone of note who needs it for 'surgical reasons'. Nathu would be quite at ease processing the animal's carcase, but he is not adept at slaughtering it. However, for one as poor as he, the money to be earned is not to be denied and he makes an endeavour to carry out the task. The scene is somewhat drawn out in order to show the stress on the unwilling butcher but also to expose the cruelty of what will soon be seen to be an unnecessary slaughter.

The man who commissions Nathu, made noticeable by his purple turban, is seen hovering in the background as the Congress hygiene party stands by, worried by the sudden clearing of the lane. Word is spread that a pig's carcase has been thrown in front of the mosque. While two of the Congress leaders sensibly go and remove the carcase from the vicinity of the mosque, this anonymous act of malicious mischief-making, designed to ignite emotions and kindle animosity, has had its desired effect which cannot be undone. Soon we see a cow being chased through a street; a little later we learn that it has been slaughtered and thrown inside a temple.

On the basis of these senseless acts of cruelty to animals, calculated for their certain communal offensiveness, the atmosphere starts to thicken with apprehension. Unseen stone-throwers and the hovering of the man with the purple turban suggest undiscerned machinations: the need to check the accessibility of the bell at the clock tower, used to alert the town to danger or emergency; the suggestion that young people should be taught skills such as fighting with lathis and even spears and swords; the advice to heat oil and coal that may be thrown at belligerent enemies; and Ranbir's father's small axe that is kept in a wardrobe are all indicative of impending violence.

In parallel to the Muslim League's quest for Pakistan, some of the young men of the Hindu community are shown being tutored on the need to establish a Hindu state and the necessity to destroy any opposition to that supposed ideal. It is here that a very significant course in the narrative is introduced out of which emanates a simple yet chilling emblematic indication of a turn towards barbarity. The seemingly innocent though intense Ranbir is being tutored by his guru, Devrath, in epic philosophy as it applies to the so-called righteous conflict.[1] The boy is told that he must have the moral strength to engage in such conflict and is put to the test by Devrath, who produces a chicken and a knife and orders Ranbir to kill the bird. Ranbir cannot bring himself to do it, nor even to watch while Devrath shows him how it is done. He is given five minutes to prove that he is worthy to be a warrior for Hinduism and he forces himself to pass the test, though bringing upon himself obvious emotional and physical distress in the process. A little later we see him with several of his fellow youth brigade members, when suddenly he is overpowered by the ambition to command and to prove his worthiness by gratuitous killing. The boy who could not bring himself to see a chicken being slaughtered now goes out into the street and senselessly stabs to death an elderly and helpless Muslim pedlar. The vile act sees him bathed in perspiration and trembling from the emotional effect of what he has done, but he has killed an 'enemy' and won the almost worshipful admiration of his comrades. In moving from chicken to elderly man, Nihalani has established a grim and frightening indication of moral descent.

So far Nihalani has been particularly adept at gradually establishing the context for the various elements of the narrative, which would not make much sense in isolation. Once again we see the man who commissioned Nathu to kill the pig; he has now changed his purple turban for a green one. From an eating-house, Nathu catches sight of him wending his way through the crowd and runs after him, apparently wanting to speak to him, but seeing Nathu the man pointedly ignores him and then deliberately evades him. His job of unexplained mischief-making has been done. It is clear that the desecration of the mosque in itself was not the reason for the dire turmoil to which this town is headed, but in the context of communal tension it was enough to set in motion acts which most rational minds under normal circumstances would never contemplate.

We have seen the emanations of friction brewing since the beginning of the film and now there is talk of the likelihood of riots and reports of tension in the town. Late at night Nathu sees a house on fire, then others, and then the clock tower bell is heard. The fire spreads and, after close shots of the flames, the partisan cries of a Hindu mob are heard as they march past the house of Karimdin, a humble and frightened Muslim schoolteacher. This is a tense and dramatic point in the film, for we might as well expect the worst; what many would not expect is that the frenzied knocking on his door (there is a close shot of the sword held in the hand of the one who is knocking) signals the presence of his Sikh neighbour, a moral giant of a woman, who has come to offer him protection. From time to time we are offered a salutary reminder that by no means were all people affected by communal blindness.

Apart from close-ups of raging flames and shots of urgent movement in the streets, Nihalani does not dwell much on the riot itself. There is very little of the graphic depiction of brutality that we see in many other Partition films; rather, we experience the riot with those who sit in awful apprehension inside their homes. Ranbir's father, Lala, is at home with his wife and daughter; they are worried about Ranbir who has not yet come home. They are also very worried for their own safety, as their house is in a Muslim locality. Lala arms his servant—a physically and intellectually disabled boy called Nanku—with a wooden post from a mosquito net frame and instructs him to guard the main door. The riot is running unchecked and cries and partisan slogans are coming from the street, so the boy is very frightened, but then his master instructs him to go out and deliver a note to his friend, Raghunath in another locality asking him to send his driver, Shahnawaz, to come and take Lala and his wife and daughter to safety.

As the boy goes out, Nihalani makes, seemingly inconsequentially, an obvious but important point. A man running for his life is being chased by three Muslims wielding lathis. He manages to get away from them, and one of the pursuers observes that no unbeliever should ever escape them again. This is a very direct way of indicating that under the lynch law, the mob imposes punishment not according to its captives' actions but according to their communal identity. A member of the Other community is guilty simply because of being that. It is such unreason that will help to explain the end of Nanku a little later.

Almost as horrible as the inferno of the night before is the scene of destruction and desolation the next morning. The flames have turned to a heavy pall of thick smoke, while small, isolated fires are still burning. Here and there, a body is lying on the ground. Carrying the Congress flag Jarnail Singh tramps down a lane and stops, aghast, to survey the horrific scene of destruction. Just then the Deputy Commissioner's open car, with the Englishman in the back seat, comes along the street. Blaming the British for the hell that has eventuated, Jarnail chases after the car crying out his condemnation of those whom he sees as the ultimate culprits and declaring his implacable opposition to the Partition. From the passion of his tirade, the poor man might seem to have lost his senses, but his words are not to be dismissed lightly. The foreign administration did have much to answer for in its arrogant and self-interested assumption of directing the course of Indian history.

It is indeed important that Jarnail Singh's anti-imperialist sentiments are not cast aside as the rantings of a madman. At a meeting of the local Socialist Party one of the men argues that it is wrong to blame the British for what he sees as a straightforward Hindu–Muslim conflict, but the Chairman replies that the vested interests of the colonial power cannot be ignored. Their divide-and-rule policies enabled them to exploit the country and provoke mayhem to their own advantage. Here we might consider the ineffectual Deputy Commissioner, whose reaction to a report of the rioting, given over a phone call that disturbs his sleep, is a wish for the people enjoying the blessings of British rule: 'Damn them. Damn them to hell!'

The end of the disabled houseboy, Nanku, comes as a consequence of the flight of his master and family. When Shahnawaz gets them to their place of refuge, Lala's wife realises that she has left her jewellery box at home. Shahnawaz goes back to get it and finds himself alone in the house with Nanku. His own Muslim identity is highlighted as he knocks on the front door, being eyed suspiciously by the residents of the Muslim neighbourhood. When he goes upstairs to the room where the box is kept, he sees through the window a Muslim funeral in the house next door, and is evidently moved by the funereal prayers. He goes out to find the innocent boy waiting for him on the stairs, and as Nanku leads the way down, Shahnawaz kicks him violently in the back, sending him flying to the floor below. The driver steps over the boy's body and goes outside to his car. While being happily employed in a Hindu home and cheerfully volunteering to help a Hindu guest does not seem to have been a problem for Shahnawaz, his presence in a Hindu house in a Muslim locality has sharpened his own sense of communal identity, making the innocent and helpless Nanku appear to him as a monstrous representative of the culpable Other.

There are two other acts of utter senselessness. One concerns Haroun Baksh, a professor of literature, also seen as emblematic of the Other by the mob who burst into his house and with true philistine contempt upset his bookshelves and set fire to his books before ransacking the rest of the house. The second is the slaying of Jarnail Singh during an impassioned public denunciation of imperialism and Partition; he takes a powerful blow to the back of the head from a lathi wielded by an unseen assailant.

Without the plethora of graphically presented violence that might be found in other Partition films, Nihalani has cogently made the point that the division of the country, in both its imminence and actuality, did generate a fall into savagery. The most prominent image is of the raging flames and the overriding implication of death and destruction, while some telling sequences of the early morning aftermath of a night of violence clearly show some of the visible consequences of the riot. After the brutal slaying of Jarnail Singh, the mayhem is shown to continue, but the treatment of it is different as confrontational realism is now avoided.

The narrative focus now falls on Nathu and his wife, Karmo. Nathu has witnessed the killing of Jarnail Singh, for which, along with all the arson, butchery and looting, he blames himself, and decides that he and Karmo must get out of the town. With their few belongings, and Nathu's mother on his back, they join the mass migration to what they assume will be safety. The flight proves to be too much for the elderly mother, who dies soon after they set out, and places tremendous strain on the heavily pregnant Karmo. Violence in one form or another travels with them. Much of it is implied through shots of their journey that show the aftermath of the rioting, as they pass by villages that have been torched, homes still smouldering and smoke mixing with the afternoon light in the forest to give a curiously mystical visual effect.

They meet up with an elderly Sikh couple, who were forced to flee their Muslim-dominated village by outsiders intent on inciting turmoil. Ironically, the old couple find themselves seeking shelter in the house of Ehsaan Ali, who turns out to have been one of the looters of their house. Ehsaan Ali wants to give them refuge but is afraid of what his son and the neighbours will do if they discover his kindness to *kafirs*. He expresses the dilemma at the core of so much of Partition violence: 'I am just giving respect to humanity. Otherwise, remembering what the kafirs have done in the city, my blood starts boiling.' The problem here is the failure to see the moral futility of revenge. There seems to be a sense of righteousness in retaliation, and if the retaliator is ever an instigator, there is somehow an element of righteousness in that too.

The Sikh couple, Harnam Singh and his wife, Banto, seek refuge in a gurudwara for themselves and Nathu and Karmo. The focus then shifts to a local disputation simmering between the Sikhs and Muslims. Meerdad, one of the Socialists we met earlier, tries to convince a leader of the Muslim community that it is all the result of the imperialists' divide-and-rule policies, but the Muslim is intent on laying the blame on the Sikhs. In the gurudwara, a peaceable and thoughtful young Sikh preaches cooperation between Sikhs and Muslims, but the more orthodox members of the congregation are intent on hostility.

The two communities do clash but we see none of it. Instead Nihalani shows us the aftermath of the conflict—desolation and destruction—and then fills in some of the details by letting us hear the prayer of one from a synthesis-seeking group, the Rababis, who are, ironically, seen by the Sikhs as Muslims, and by the Muslims as Sikhs. The indirect representation of the riot is an effective alternative to realistic depiction, and the significance of the implication of religious synthesis is remarkably thought-provoking in this context.

Train to Pakistan

Pamela Rooks' *Train to Pakistan* (1998) is a sensibly restrained film, like Khushwant Singh's novel of the same name on which it is based. The mayhem into which one Punjabi village eventually descends is clearly and economically presented, while the notion of descent *from* is carefully examined and with good purpose. Such a film can hardly have a happy ending, but this one ends at least with a redeeming assertion of good over the forces of moral blindness.

Two interesting suggestions are made early in the film. During the titles sequence there is a flashback in which a little boy sees his father about to be hanged in a British Indian jail. This moves into a brief passage of explanatory commentary by the present District Magistrate, Hukum Chand, which then moves into a scene in which two rival Sikh gangs meet ostensibly to bury the hatchet but, in fact, to let treachery loose and fan the flames of antagonism. The hanging—or state-initiated violence—has not put a stop to banditry, acrimonious rivalry or arbitrary killing; indeed, given the power of easily engendered resentment to propagate itself along with criminal behaviour, the state might even be thought of as a cause of the often sorry predicament of those whom it claims to govern.

The second suggestion, which emerges at the beginning of the film and is substantiated throughout, would have us imagine that the now well-known, stereotypical violence of the Partition did not erupt simultaneously and uniformly throughout India or even in one particular province. People in different places from varying backgrounds did not react in accordance with any particular pattern. Moreover, the suggestion in this film is that the urge to havoc is sometimes caused by the malicious contrivance of outsiders. If animosity does not exist, then it has to be invented.

Soon after the film begins the District Magistrate makes a claim which he will reiterate more than once as the narrative progresses. He asserts that his district is a peaceful one, an assertion that is credible though amusingly ironic, given his own volatile personality and proneness to erupt into turbulent fits of ill temper when displeased. He declares that Hindus, Muslims and Sikhs all live in harmony in the district; the film gives no evidence to the contrary, though the mischief of bandit gangs is evident early and throughout, and this would seem to be the major cause of headache for the police and the judiciary.

An unwitting emblem of communal harmony comes to this village of Mano Majra in the person of a young Communist worker called Iqbal. There is a hint of enigma about him for his full name, as the police inspector points out, might be Iqbal Chand, making him a Hindu, or Iqbal Mohammed, making him Muslim, or Iqbal Singh, so corroborating his later claim to be a Sikh. His circumcision, ascertained during a clumsy and quite unnecessary police examination, might complicate matters, though his explanation that it was carried out in England after an infection would seem to be credible. What is evident is that Iqbal shows no antipathy to anyone other than the police for unjustly arresting and detaining him. In conversation with the elderly Sikh leader of the gurudwara, he learns that the village is made up largely of Sikhs, but there are Muslims there too—and 'we all look after one another'. At the mosque he learns something of interest to him, given his Marxist outlook, which is that the Sikhs are mostly landlords and that the Muslims are mostly peasants. Any seeds of conflict of interest to a revolutionary would be found in this class distinction which presents itself, incidentally, in communal terms. However, he is also assured that the notion of conflict is remote. Indeed, even after the winds of malice have been thoroughly fanned, the Sikhs turn out in huge numbers to bid an emotional farewell to their Muslim 'brothers and sisters' as they are evacuated for their safety to a refugee camp. Some may even be heartened by the Magistrate's naive belief, which the Inspector only partly corrects, that it will all blow over in a week and things will again be like they always were.

The suggestion of darkening tomorrows might be discerned in the shot of a train, overcrowded and with many riding on the roof, crossing the frame from right to left. The slogans being shouted are pro-India so we may assume that refugees from Pakistan are coming to East or Indian Punjab. The old and purblind weaver is a little perturbed that the trains seem to be running at all hours now and with no apparent schedule. The dancing girl, Hasina, tells Hukum Chand that in the town—Chandernagore—it is unsafe for Muslims to venture out of their homes. Then comes the worst of it: the trains are now arriving with all their passengers slaughtered. There is a horrible scene in which the Magistrate and the Inspector enter a carriage to find a tangled mass of dead and bloodied bodies; the two men choke as they hold handkerchiefs to their faces, indicating the overpowering stench of rotting flesh. The army sends in a unit to see to the cremations of the dead, and the residents of Mano Majra are enjoined to supply firewood and kerosene for the purpose. Then refugee groups are seen coming from afar, carrying bundles and wending their way through the fields. There is a cut to a shot of the huge pyres burning and soon we will see the smoke rising up and darkening the sky.

While it is obvious that most of the villagers seem immune to the evolving animosity, some of the Sikh soldiers who have come as part of the cremation unit are openly discourteous and even hostile to the local Muslims; indeed, those entrusted with keeping the peace are actually efficacious in giving rise to acrimony and notions of vengeance. Then, before the trucks can take the Muslims to the refugee camp, the purblind mullah's house is broken into by Sikh thugs, apparently from elsewhere, and he is cruelly assaulted by them. After the convoy has left for the camp, the thugs go on a rampage of looting and burning.

Someone catches the horrible sight of bodies floating down the river and alerts the others. The cremations begin again. And then the Sikh thugs taunt the local congregation in the gurudwara, calling them a 'bunch of eunuchs', trying to incite hatred against the Muslims. They offer only one moral imperative—what they see as the ethic of revenge: 'If they kill one of us, we'll kill two of them; if they rape one of our women, we'll rape two of theirs.' The simple imputation of righteousness to the sterile emotion of revenge now gives sanction and free rein to rape and murder. An old man asks what bravery there is in killing innocent people, but revenge has blinded the protagonist of malice to what the questioner is actually asking. The reply is a stubborn and irrelevant counter-question: 'What about the children of Hindus and Sikhs killed before their parents' eyes? Weren't they innocent?'

The avengers' plan is then disclosed. The next night a train filled with Muslims will cross the bridge for Pakistan, and those on board should meet with the same fate to which they subjected the Sikhs and Hindus. There is obviously a flaw in this thinking, based on a conflation of the *they* who will be on that train with another *they* of another time and another place. Moreover, that train will be coming from Chandernagore, carrying all the Muslims who had lived in this village of Mano Majra as brothers and sisters and who are guilty of nothing. It is Jagat Singh's deadly rival, Malli, who is first to respond to the call.

The District Magistrate, now ready to try anything, and knowing that his Hasina, the dancing girl, will be on the train, orders the release of Jagat Singh (who is in love with Nooran, the daughter of the purblind Mullah) and Iqbal, whom he now recognises as Iqbal Singh. As they are being brought in a tonga from the jail to the village they are apprised of the plan to attack the train. A rope will be hung across the line low enough to sweep off all those sitting on the roof of the train, some three or four hundred, dashing them to the ground where they will be slaughtered. Gunmen will be there to shoot at the windows as well.

There are shots of the crowd at Chandernagore station swarming into the train and onto its roof, among them Nooran and her father and the District Magistrate's Hasina. There are then shots of the armed thugs lying low along the track. There is a shot of Jagat Singh, ne'er-do-well son of a hanged ne'er-do-well, about to climb up to the rope which is already set in place. The camera tilts up to show him on high trying to cut through the thick and heavy rope. The train is getting closer. The rope is cut just as Malli shoots at Jagat and he plummets to the ground. The train goes on to Pakistan, its passengers none the wiser of a failed atrocity. The atrocity failed because of the self-sacrifice of the film's anti-hero: the son of a man hanged by the rope of the foreign rulers loses his life cutting the would-be lethal rope put in place by extremists of his own community.

Train to Pakistan focuses clearly and rationally on the gradual disintegration of harmonious co-existence along with the gradual growth of virulent and irrational vengefulness. The film is very strong in its representation of what certainly or probably did happen. It is made all the more thought-provoking by its metaphors of cross-cultural empathy: in the character of Iqbal who identifies as one with the many through the international workers' movement; in the relationship of the high official, Hukum Chand and the insignificant dancing girl, Hasina; and in the true love between Nooran, the daughter of the purblind mullah and the criminal son of a hanged criminal, Jagat Singh, the saviour of thousands.

Earth

For her 1998 film, *Earth,* Deepa Mehta found inspiration in Bapsi Sidhwa's acclaimed novel, *Ice-Candy-Man* (1991). The film is a worthy endeavour to portray macrocosmic notions of the Partition of India through the microcosm of a group of friends bonded together by a beautiful young woman, Shanta, and her responsibility and affection for a little girl crippled by polio, Lenny baby. The broader canvas of a divided country is hinted at soon after the opening of the film when Lenny drops a plate on the floor. It does not break conveniently into three pieces that might suggest India and the two wings of Pakistan, but shatters into many pieces, suggesting the wholesale disintegration of country, community, society, family, and even the individual to whom the Partition gave birth. The film's focal microcosm, however, is the group of friends who meet regularly, until the Partition has unleashed the dreadful and incomprehensible barbarities that render the happy group to the state of a china plate dropped upon the floor.

Even in 1947, the idea of partition was unthinkable for many. A worried Shanta, Lenny's nursemaid, asks the little girl's mother if it is true that a huge canal is to be dug to separate one country from the other. Later, Lenny's parents, Parsis, host a dinner party at which seeds of conflict germinate. An arrogant Englishman and an aggressive Sikh almost come to blows, and a preview of the problems is presented: the authenticity or otherwise of the perceived reasons for division, the settling of differences, and the blaming of the English for India's problems including the introduction of venereal diseases into the country. The Englishman expresses grave doubts in India's capacity for self-rule, doubts that will perhaps be justified for a short time at least.

By contrast, we meet Shanta's group of friends in the park. They are a social mix—two Hindus, three Muslims, a Sikh, and little Lenny, a Parsi—and are evidently presented as an emblematic miniature of the wider society. As a group they function harmoniously, taking obvious joy in each other's company and offering mutual care and support. However, underneath the surface of this happy society there is the potential for conflict. While all, especially Lenny, hold Shanta in close affection, Shanta is loved by two men. It would have been too obvious to have made one a Hindu and the other a Muslim, and so, shunning that clichéd and trite symbolism, both suitors are Muslims and the narrative dynamics are driven by personalities, not by communal stylising.

While the members of the group are aware of the communal tension, they feel no desire to talk about it. Dilnawaz makes it plain that 'we are all people, the same. What difference is there between Hindu and Muslim?' And yet it seems that politicised communalism is a growing cancer. There is a sequence in which Lenny and her parents are driving through a narrow lane of the city and confront a large demonstration coming towards them, carrying green and white flags and shouting pro-Pakistan and anti-India slogans. The car has to stop and wait for the demonstrators to pass by, many of them showing their disdain and hostility by climbing onto the bonnet and walking over the top of the car, and some of them gleefully kicking the windscreen as they go. Mehta is careful to present such antagonistic elements gradually and not allow the possibility that this frenzied display is in any way prefabricated. The demonstrators also appear unexpectedly, making their sudden appearance somewhat inexplicable. On the other hand the friends in the park are perplexed at the notion that things have changed to the unthinkable position that Hindus, Muslims and Sikhs should live separately from one another.

However, even the group of friends senses ripples of discord. The sometimes madcap Dilnawaz (Lenny's 'Ice-Candy-wallah') appears one day as a crazy Sufi fakir, overacting the role hilariously. He carries a disconnected telephone handset by which he 'enables' troubled souls to make direct contact with Allah. A somewhat earnest Sikh among the onlookers questions the value of Dilnawaz's telephone, sparking a hostile response from a similarly earnest Muslim man. The situation is diffused by Dilnawaz, who accepts someone's request to call Allah and ask what things will be like after Independence. He informs them, both humorously and ominously, that 'Allah says that at the time of the division there will arise a huge storm and all of you will fight like animals. Now I must go. I've got an appointment with Mr Jinnah.'

One senses that the tensions brewing in the country are inevitably affecting Shanta and her friends. Over a meal together in a local eating-house, tension develops between the Muslim butcher and the Sikh zoo attendant, prompting Hasan, Dilnawaz's rival for Shanta, to offer some heartfelt hope: 'For ages we have lived like brothers. Our language is the same. Our enemies are the same. Sikhs came into being to bring Hindus and Muslims together. And why fight among friends? We will stand by each other, won't we?' The response to his question is a very lukewarm affirmative, seemingly without conviction. Noble sentiment would seem to have been devalued.

Another element of partition reality is introduced unexpectedly. On his way through the lanes of the city, Hasan sees for the first time an unmistakable departure of émigrés, people with glum faces looking down, carrying bundles and boxes, some men with sticks driving bullock carts bearing precious furniture, faces marked by fear, some tear-stained, some still crying, and the camera drifts into a long shot to reveal that the column of fugitives is indeed lengthy and populous. It is an extended shot, almost without dialogue and truly moving in its impact. Then there is a cut from this general scene to a particular one. Surinder, the Sikh at the dinner party earlier in the film, and his wife come to say goodbye to Lenny's parents. There is mention of mutual friends, Sikh and Hindu, who have already left or intend to leave soon. Surinder is bitter, blaming the British for cutting up his country and distributing the pieces like playing cards, while the lines on a map drawn by an Englishman are now coming between him and his friends.

By now Mehta has done enough to allow mayhem to embrace this group of good and innocent friends. She takes time in establishing the crescendo of tension that will bring it about, but significantly she chooses to set it against the backdrop of night. On a dimly lit railway station, Dilnawaz sits waiting for a train bringing his sisters as fugitives from India. But he is utterly unprepared for the gruesome sight that confronts him when he boards the train to look for them. At first he sees, touches and smells a profusion of blood; then the camera moves over a mass of hideously distorted, mutilated and bloodied bodies, male and female, young and old. We learn later that no one on the overcrowded train was spared this hellish brutality nor the perversion of its perpetrators—four sacks full of women's breasts were found among the corpses.

Until now Dilnawaz has been prominent, though incidental to the narrative, as the face of optimism, joy and laughter. Now he becomes focal, and we note a readily understandable yet sinister change coming over him. Shanta and Lenny come to meet him on his rooftop; he is pensive, perhaps brooding. There is some commotion in the streets below. We see a shot of shouting, torch-bearing Sikhs rushing through the lanes below and confronting an armed contingent of police. 'What are these bloody turbans doing here?,' snarls Dilnawaz, an expression that would have been hitherto very much out of character for him. Fighting breaks out as the police try to drive the mob back. Men from other communities join the melee. One man is captured by the mob and each of his legs is tied to a different retreating police car, both moving in opposite directions; fortunately we do not see the culmination of this appalling act of savagery. The shouting now indicates that Muslims are dominating the riot and that revenge is being carried out for the slaughter on the train. From the rooftop, the Hindu quarter of the city can be seen going up in flames. There are explosions and Dilnawaz observes, 'There goes the dynamite the Hindus had stacked for us.' A fire engine comes close and firemen are seen dousing the nearby houses with petrol. Dilnawaz notes that they must be Muslims and a hint of a smile comes to his face; Shanta is visibly alarmed. There are shots of panic-stricken people in the street, some of them ablaze.

Dilnawaz indulges in a moment of philosophy, telling Shanta that it is not about different communities, but about everyone. 'We're all demons, all beasts.' He asks her to marry him so that 'the beast inside me will stay on a leash.' It is easy to write off the fall into barbarism, claiming it to be innate to everyone. However, Hasan a little later, and Imam Din later still, will bear out the lie in Dilnawaz's justification of human savagery. And we do not know what the young man tied to the police jeeps did to warrant dismemberment; probably his crime was merely being there.

It is a common truism that evil will flourish when good people do nothing to prevent it. This bothers Lenny's mother, who is concerned that their neutrality means a failure to support their friends. Her husband sees it as a moral dilemma as he asks, 'Hindu, Muslim, Sikh—whom do we not betray?' It is indeed true that in some cases to support one means to fail another; however, Hasan quite clearly is no less a Muslim despite his sheltering the Sikh Sher Singh and his family. It only makes his own brutal murder all the more heinous.

The focus is back on Lenny for a short, very touching sequence, in which she and her young friend make contact with a little Muslim boy who is temporarily camped beside her house with a group of fugitive women, probably victims of rape. Lenny prompts him to report that their village was attacked by a mob of Hindus who killed everyone, though he escaped by hiding under the dead bodies. After the brutes had left, he went looking for his mother. He found her in a mosque tied by her hair to a ceiling fan. Lenny is visibly affected by this boy's tragic experience, for the dismemberment of the young man in the street riot has also affected her deeply, as reflected in her seemingly perverse act of ripping apart one of her stuffed dolls and collapsing into tears.

So much of the Partition violence was like an endless vendetta: one violent act incurred another in retaliation, which in turn set in process a chain of revenge, that sterile, negative emotion that the morally bankrupt see as a justification for, rather than a causal element of, the entire catastrophe. Dilnawaz remarks that Sher Singh has apparently vanished (we learn a little later that he is being secretly sheltered by Hasan), and it is a good thing for him to get away from the riots 'that the Sikhs have started'. He points out that the Muslim refugees from India are bent on revenge and he confesses to lobbing bombs into Hindu homes. 'For each of my sisters' breasts I want to kill all the bastards.' There is further opportunity for Dilnawaz to indulge in his lust for vengeance. Shanta will agree to marry Hasan, and Hasan's body, naked, bloodied and wrapped in sacking, will be found on the street. Shanta, too, will pay for her love.

The savagery and destruction we have seen so far has been perpetrated at night. There is a simple symbolism in evil being embraced by the darkness, aside from the visual reality that infernal flames are more striking against the backdrop of a black sky. Now, in the bright light of day, we see the wickedness that ends this chapter in Lenny's life. The daylight exposes the moral sterility of the self-righteous mob who come to the Parsis' house demanding that the Hindus there be handed over to them. Hatiya has converted to Islam to save himself and claims now to be Himmat Ali. He is humiliated by being obliged to publicly prove his conversion by displaying his circumcision. We note that it is another Muslim, Imam Din, the Parsis' servant, who stands in moral outrage between Himmat Ali and the mob led, ironically though unsurprisingly, by the butcher from our once joyous group of friends, and who now demands that the Hindu nanny be brought out. And then Dilnawaz arrives. Lenny runs to him as to a saviour, and in enacting the role that was once his nature, he picks her up and asks where her nanny is; Lenny, as though bearing out the concern earlier expressed by her father, unwittingly betrays Shanta. The enraged and lustful mob drag out the screaming, terrified young woman. No one can save her. The elderly Imam Din is knocked to the ground and the thugs walk over him. Shanta is taken away in a cart, followed by the pack of wild dogs who once were men. In the sunshine their perversity, their swinishness and their unrestrained brutality can find nowhere to hide or even to appear less manifest.

The film might well have ended there and been powerful in its impact. However, that impact is diluted somewhat by an unnecessary epilogue. The scene is a barren park with many pedestals, statues of imperial personages remaining on some of them, but the rest devoid of sculpture. Even Queen Victoria lies prone in the dust. It is 50 years after the Partition, and a crippled old woman gets up and questions what the Partition had achieved and to bemoan the fact that in betraying her nanny, she lost a part of herself. Even there the film might have ended well, but there follows a long reprise of what look like highlight scenes, with no apparent purpose.

Earth is a worthy and confronting depiction of the violence and atrocity that arose out of the propaganda of the time, as well as a plausible representation of the corrupting of human relations spurred on by the horrible adult emotion of vengeance. The communally mixed group of friends make good cinematic sense as symbolic of the communally mixed nation, and the significance of Dilnawaz, the most likeable character for most of the film, becoming the treacherous, satanic villain at the end, is disturbing and disquietingly thought-provoking. Perhaps the greatest sadness to linger on 50 years after the turmoil is the corrupting of Lenny, culminating in her unwitting betrayal of Shanta. The part of herself that she lost was her innocence, and in that she is emblematic of an entire generation.

The presentation of mayhem in *Earth* proceeds out of the presentation of its opposite, and so we make whatever sense we can of it from what precedes it. Of course, the previous condition is not absolute; there are indeed ripples on the tranquil surface, hints that something here and there is amiss, and, as fear and apprehension take hold, a realisation gradually develops that something awful and inexplicable is happening, seemingly inexorably.

Hey Ram

Such a binary view is not followed in all other films dealing with the Partition, and in some the mayhem is presented as an actuality isolated from any concern for accountability and manifests itself as a stage in nothing of any special or major significance. Multifarious violence is presented as an agent of change, without the question *from what?* being addressed with much interest; the question *to what?* is probably the stuff of other films. This kind of arbitrary depiction of communal strife is germane to Kamal Haasan's *Hey Ram*[2] (2000), a very long film that tries to do far too much and ultimately becomes a cluttered mess of narrative meanderings and patchwork ideas. Its presentation of violence is characteristic of popular cinema, seemingly intended more to entertain than to enlighten. Nevertheless, its representation of the dreadful violence that made a hell of Calcutta for some days after Jinnah's Direct Action Day (16 August 1946) would seem to be in accord with candid accounts given by historians.[3] The purpose of this cinematic account of the Direct Action violence is simply to provide the crisis that sets its central character on the long and convoluted narrative path that forms the rest of the film.

Saket Ram is an archaeologist working with the renowned Sir Mortimer Wheeler on excavating the Indus Valley Civilisation in what is soon to become Pakistan. The unrest surrounding the imminence of the Partition puts a halt to their work and Saket returns to his wife in Calcutta. On the way to his house his taxi is besieged by a mob of Muslim demonstrators agitating wildly for Pakistan, and a title card tells us that the date is 16 August 1946. However, no card tells us that the date is that of the so-called Direct Action Day declared by Jinnah to give a spirited fillip to his campaign for Pakistan. In fact, Jinnah and Direct Action are not given substantial mention at all, nor is any elucidation provided of the partition controversy. There is simply the unrest in the streets, apparently self-generated.

Saket gets home and scenes of marital flippancy and mild eroticism are stretched out almost beyond endurance before he goes out to try to purchase some food. He is soon caught up with disorder again, and is able to rescue a girl being pursued by a maddened Muslim mob. Perhaps this is a semiotic suggestion of what is to follow, for he then returns home to find the house being attacked by a group of Muslim thugs. He is bound, beaten and held while some of the men rape his wife, Aparna. He has an altercation with his guard and is able to break free, sending the guard over the balcony. The police arrive, Saket Ram fires some shots with his revolver, and then he sees that his wife has been attacked with a knife and is bleeding profusely. She dies, and Saket Ram is frenzied.

There is a cut to outside the house, where buildings are on fire and crowds are rampaging through the blazing streets. Evidently maddened, Saket Ram is among them, his revolver in hand. What seems like a kangaroo court is in progress and some men are taken and thrown into a burning building. Then Saket Ram confronts one of his wife's attackers, a tailor called Altaf. He was a part of the demonstration that besieged Saket Ram's taxi when he was on the way home; he had recognised Saket Ram and respectfully greeted him and helped him through the crowd. However, they met again when Altaf was part of the group who raped and killed Aparna. Now, without his accomplices and facing an enraged, newly bereaved and armed Saket Ram, he is obliged to submit to his mercy. Here we have a clear, albeit contrived, example of the radical changes that might be wrought in someone under the influence of mob frenzy. It is not just Altaf who is overwhelmed by moral decline but also Saket Ram. Saket Ram has no mercy for Altaf and shoots him without a thought; he then turns around and shoots another Muslim. Deranged violence has claimed the civilised scholar of antiquity, just as an old man is seen being ruthlessly stabbed by a younger one.

Saket Ram meets a group of men wearing the characteristic black caps of the RSS, along with their leader, Sriram Abhayankar. Here an element of rationale is provided for Saket Ram's burgeoning odyssey of reprisal to bolster the angry vengeance provoked by his wife's rape and murder. Abhayankar gives Saket Ram a paper, asks him to read it, and to come and meet him sometime. Saket Ram then goes on his way, buildings and vehicles blazing all around him, as a group of Sikhs behead a Muslim man.

In the early light of the next morning, the gardens around the Victoria Memorial are seen strewn with bodies and vultures are circling overhead. The streets are scenes of chaotic destruction. Fires are still smouldering and a man hangs by his neck from a tree. A police van filled with corpses goes by and a tethered elephant is gently restive as its mahout lies dead and bloodied at its feet. In this atmosphere Saket Ram meets Abhayankar and confesses his distress, guilt and shame at having sunk to the level of a murderer. Abhayankar tells him that 20 men raped and killed his sister, bewailing the horror suffered by 'so many mothers, so many sisters.' He tells Saket Ram that his actions were 'not crimes but duties.' Then comes the element of rationale. Abhayankar seeks to attribute blame for this terrible carnage. With a word he absolves Jinnah, the general of Direct Action, and his faithful lieutenant, the Premier of Bengal, Suhrawardy (who later in the film admits, with some historical validity, his responsibility for much of the carnage). Abhayankar lays the blame squarely at the feet of the apostle of non-violence, Mohandas Karamchand Gandhi! The righteous assassination of Gandhi now becomes Saket Ram's obsession.

It is difficult to determine which claim is more extraordinary, that of Jinnah's innocence or that of Gandhi's guilt. No argument is given by Abhayankar to support his claim, but Saket Ram—the educated, scholarly archaeologist—accepts it implicitly.

Later in the film he will accept just as implicitly the goodness of Gandhi. Through an orgy of violence Saket Ram comes to the Gandhian side, not through the force of truth as we might have expected of a scholar but through a long lesson learned from the experience of irrational vengeance. While the depiction of the barbarity of Direct Action in Calcutta would seem quite plausible, given the accounts of respected historians, in general the mayhem of *Hey Ram* has very little to explain it. Presented in such a vacuum, it too often appears as the violence of ghoulish titillation rather than the violence of actuality.

Gandhi, *Sardar* and *Viceroy's House* revisited

The films discussed in Chapter 1—*Gandhi*, *Sardar* and *Viceroy's House*—are relatively wide-ranging in content, especially *Gandhi* and *Sardar*, and the barbarity emanating from the Partition is treated as part of broadly conceived and carefully detailed narratives. While the ferocious tumult is by no means minimised, it is incidental to more encompassing issues. Nevertheless, the treatments are significant.

Attenborough's film, focussing on an exceptional man and his role in history, does not show much of the violence that accompanied Partition. However, one scene does represent very effectively the notions of blame and retaliation. It shows two trails of refugees passing each other, one headed west and the other going eastward. The first shot is a circular panoramic high shot indicating the immensity of the numbers in each procession. Some medium shots show what might have been an unusually large number of carts and pack animals, mostly camels, though a majority of the refugees are on foot, carrying whatever they can. Close shots show faces numbed by devastation and resigned to hardship. A woman carrying a baby comes into close shot; the baby's head is bandaged and the bandage is bloody. The woman hands the baby to its father; apparently the infant is dead. The father is overwhelmed with grief, and that emotion turns quickly into helpless rage as he watches representatives of the Other going in the opposite direction. He returns the baby to his wife and runs into the no-man's land between the two columns of refugees, picks up some stones and throws them at the opposite line. In no time, hundreds are overwhelmed by the distorted notions of Otherness and a horrible conflict ensues.

It might be tempting to point out the likely unreality of such a meeting of two huge columns of refugees, but this would be to miss the point which, put simply, concerns basic human helplessness. The man who starts the brawl is not malicious, he is not a mischief-maker, he is not a hate-filled fanatic. He is one of a vast number of bereaved fathers (or husbands or brothers or sons) who have been through, and are still trying to survive, unimaginable nightmares. He might sense but cannot articulate a mammoth injustice in the death of his child; he cannot blame the culprit, who is probably unknown, and so he takes out his frustration on the culprit's co-religionists. His attack with stones is irrational; it is urged by inefficacy, not by spite.

Attenborough's other representation of Partition mayhem is set on the opposite side of the country in the great metropolis of Calcutta. Riots had erupted in various parts of India but the tumult in Calcutta was particularly intense. We see a high shot of the city at night, looking from the east across the rooftops toward the Howrah Bridge. Many of the buildings are lit by electric lights but many are also lit by flames. Police are seen trying to restore order where an unruly mob have set fire to a car. Men are patrolling the streets in groups, many of them bearing flaming torches. A Hindu mob gathers outside the house in the Muslim locality where Gandhi is staying, fasting until death, and raise the chant, 'Death to Muslims!' Members of the crowd voice their hostility toward Gandhi, condemning him for staying in a Muslim house, for 'Muslims killed my family!' as one of them cries, someone in whose mind the question of Hindus killing Muslim families perhaps does not arise.

There is a cut to the next day and we see a tram commandeered by police bulldozing the rubble of furniture and other broken items along a street. The police get out and confront a brawling crowd—men fighting furiously with lathis and throwing stones, with bodies strewn here and there. The police open fire and disperse the crowd. Night falls and the rioting does not abate. A group of Muslim women are dragged from a car, presumably to be abused; the car is then bashed, overturned and set on fire. In the wild brawl a man is viciously stabbed. The frenzy is unrestrained.

Mob fury such as this, particularly in a city famous for its writers, poets, painters and musicians, is indeed frightening. The disquieting point is made with great force and is not laboured. The unruliness does continue, but more in the context of the assassination narrative (the face of Nathuram Godse is shown among the mob outside the house where Gandhi is staying) than in regard to the Partition.

Ketan Mehta, in *Sardar*, has more to say about the mayhem. Generally the representations are realistic, rational and restrained, but once or twice the urge to be technically spectacular has not been resisted (for example, one shot of a beheading, meant to be horrible, turns out to be ludicrously gruesome).

To show the full impact of Jinnah's bullying for Pakistan we are shown some images of the effects his menacing call for Direct Action had in Calcutta. This section opens with some black-and-white documentary footage of crowds demonstrating in the street before a newspaper headline reports the killing of more than 90 people in the city in one day. There is more archival film of furniture being burnt in the street, a burnt out bus, corpses lying in a lane, a burnt out car, smouldering buildings and rubble strewn throughout a desolate street. There is a headline concerning military firing on rioters and then a chilling statistic, '1000 Feared Dead in Calcutta'. Direct Action Day lasted nearly a week in the city at a tremendous cost of human life and property. The true nature of Jinnah's strong-arm endeavour comes with authoritative force through Mehta's careful use of file footage and newspaper headlines.

Immediately following on the shots of the mass jubilation of Independence Day, highlighting the fact that jubilation was cruelly compromised, there is a shot of a rural street; a horse-drawn cart with one wheel on fire and its canopy ablaze comes into the frame. The horse rears up in fright, the cart overturns and its two occupants tumble onto the ground just as a gang of men wielding swords and sticks come running down the street, some picking out a quarry and giving chase. There is hand-to-hand combat, one man is beheaded and another brutally stabbed; someone is set on fire and thrown from a rooftop. Fire has broken out here and there and the open space is soon littered with bodies. There is a wild melee of hacking, slashing and beating, and in the midst of this a terrified woman runs and jumps into a well. Men are seen making off with cattle and other property, one man is carrying a struggling, panic-stricken woman. In the light of the spreading fires a man is seen hanging from the branch of a tree. As night starts to fall spot fires are still burning and corpses are strewn all over the road and in the midst of all this a naked toddler cries for its mother. As though to authenticate it all headlines scream out the actuality of 'Riot and Destruction in Punjab', 'Orgy of Violence and Plunder in Lahore', and there is reference to the active work of armed gangs in Punjab and the total destruction of a number of villages around Amritsar.

It was not only Punjab, riots crippled the capital too. There is a shot of a crowd of Muslims near the Red Fort, some bearing black flags, rushing towards the camera. Clouds of dust are raised as rickshaws and carts are overturned. There is a cut to another lane and we see wholesale looting of shops. A man is pushed over a balcony railing and he falls to the street below while a butcher is beheaded on his own block. Bloodied bodies lie here and there, burning starts and goods are thrown out onto the street. Some policemen stand idly by, helpless to do anything against the great force of numbers. One of the miscreants declares that Muslims are responsible for all this turmoil for it was they who 'robbed us and raped our women', oblivious of the fact that retaliation only protracts the mayhem and enhances its barbarity. Headlines tell us of the imposition of a 12-hour curfew in Delhi and that refugees have been warned about breaching the peace (refugees were particularly prone to exacting vengeance given the horrors that so many of them had suffered in the places from where they had been driven away). This scene of devastation ends with shots of a smoky lane, almost deserted except for a few policemen, some stretcher-bearers, and a man dousing a fire.

More than most of the films dealing with the Partition, *Sardar* is candid in showing the depths of the depravity of violence visited upon people who were uninformed and utterly unprepared for the inevitable and the imagined implications of the division of the country. Ketan Mehta's sense of proportion is notable in melding his depiction of the turmoil with the greater narrative and the arguments that are woven throughout its development.

In *Viceroy's House*, the descent into mayhem is first seen in the vice-regal palace itself. There are instances of the vast army of servants overhearing snatches of conversation between Mountbatten and one Indian leader or another. At first the reactions to the mention of partition or Pakistan is an expression on a servant's face, but then a little later a conversation amongst a group of servants becomes heated with the mention of partition provoking an impassioned 'Pakistan zindabad!' proposed by one and supported vociferously by several others. Some newsreel film is shown in the palace to the viceroy's personal staff and some servants, giving illustrated reports of riots in the country's northwest and Punjab. There are some very graphic shots of death and destruction, and the human misery on-screen is complemented by the concern and compassion on the faces of some of the servants seen in close-up. Then we see a big gathering of servants outside a room where Mountbatten is trying to persuade Gandhi to accept the Partition plan. The mention of division prompts subdued utterances of 'zindabad' for Pakistan from some. This soon becomes heated as the blame for violence is somewhat arbitrarily asserted by some of the servants. A few have to be physically restrained or kept apart. Even some of the security guards are seen manhandling one another. One of the viceroy's English staff is spat on and the security guards refuse the officer's order to escort the offender out. Acrimony and unruliness are now seen to exist openly in the heart of the imperial power.

Gurinder Chadha creates a narrative of the dispelling of restraint and civility in the viceroy's house. She also uses the authenticity of black-and-white newsreel footage to depict the actual rioting, showing mob violence with loss of life, arson and looting. In addition she recreates scenes of turmoil to enhance the narrative, such as when Aalia and Jeet search frantically for Aalia's father in the midst of raging fires. The violence is also tempered by its being indirectly presented, such as the newspaper report of the train massacre which causes Jeet great distress in his concern for Aalia and her father. And at the end of the film there are the innumerable stories of horror, told by implication, in Chadha's depiction of the reality of the refugee camps. She does not exploit violence as morbid entertainment, she does not sensationalise; all is offered with measured restraint.

Partition revisited

Vic Sarin's *Partition* has been discussed in the previous chapter. However, it is of interest here for the particular light that it sheds on the virally obsessive fixation with revenge. A long trail of many, many Muslim refugees is seen wending its way to Pakistan. As in all the countless other images of refugees on the march, documented or represented, they are shown to be humble people, resigned to hardship, possessing little and carrying it on their heads or in their hands; some have the luxury of a dray or the back of an animal; some are bringing their goats with them. Suddenly a band of sword-wielding Sikhs on horseback swoop down on them. People are wildly slashed, stabbed or hacked; one man is set ablaze. Belongings are abandoned and families and friends are separated as they disperse, running amok in panic. In the horrible melee, an elderly man is stabbed and killed by a Sikh lustfully chasing after a young woman. There is just enough of this violence to make the audience appalled at what otherwise sane, decent people can sink to; then there is a shot of the desolation after the attack. There is a very telling shot of a blind man, who has been separated from his carer, wandering helplessly through the bodies strewn over the ground and calling out to him. Dead animals lie among the slaughtered men, women and children. There is a lovely shot of a mother lulling her baby, followed by a pathetic one of a baby trying to feed off the breast of its evidently dead mother.

There is a credible endeavour to give some kind of rationale to this horror. The narrative turns to Avtar, one of the leaders of the raid, chiding Gyan for not taking part in it. Gyan protests that it was an attack on innocent people, as, of course, it was. Avtar rejects this, however, stating, 'They got what they deserved.' This is simply self-righteous arrogance. Communal lynch mobs always justify their brutality by blaming it on the victims. Just how righteous their mission was can be seen when Gyan goes out to his field and sees the men dispatched to clear away the bodies, chatting and laughing as they go about their gruesome work. However, some substance might then be attached to Avtar's bitter sententiousness as he informs Gyan that a train has arrived from Pakistan. There is a shot of the sky with vultures circling and then shots of a train full of dead bodies, all of them smeared and dripping with blood, cloaked in silence; the roof of the train bears witness to more of the same butchery. To Avtar this would serve to justify beyond the slightest moral qualm the revenge mission of the previous day; but people like Gyan might point out that those killed the previous day were not responsible for the slaughter on the train. Moreover, for Gyan this cycle of violence and vengefulness is without end, for a close friend of his mother has lost her family on that train and Gyan's mother is buoyed by hatred; the girl in Gyan's house being protected as a fugitive from the massacre of the previous day would also like to see her mother and family again. Then we hear on the radio news that looting and rioting are continuing, that thousands of people near the border have been slaughtered, and that Amritsar and Lahore are burning.

We are not given a diluted presentation of the horrors dealt with in this part of the film, nor is the savagery exaggerated. It is an intelligent and persuasive endeavour to relate the action of horror to the powerful yet base emotion of revenge.

47 to 84

Rajeev Sharma's film, *47 to 84. Hun Main Kisnu Watan Kahunga* ('47 to 84. Where is My Country?', 2014) deals with both the Partition and the anti-Sikh riots following the assassination of Indira Gandhi, the then Prime Minister of India, in 1984. The latter is discussed in a later chapter, but the opening section of the film, dealing with the Partition, offers a simple representation of the process from peaceful and happy co-existence through the deliberately perpetrated butchery to forced emigration. Much of these 20 or so minutes is very filmy, elaborating what might be entertaining for some and minimising what might have been food for thought for many. A title card sets the time and place: *Undivided Punjab. August, 1947*, and so the claim is clearly made that in the days prior to Partition, one part of India at least enjoyed communal harmony. Of course, the Partition had been a probability for some time and, since the announcement of the Mountbatten Plan on 3 June 1947, a certainty. That explains the widespread unrest spreading throughout the country over months, a social disintegration that apparently bypassed the film's particular region of 'undivided Punjab'.

The first scene is set in a Sikh *akhara* where men are engaged in physical exercise. There is not much point to this other than to emphasise the bond between a father and his daughter, Sukhmani, the narrator and central character of the film. Weaponry is used but only as an aide to physical discipline; nevertheless, it does allude to Sikh militancy. There is then a brief narrative detail concerning a Muslim merchant supplying cloth for a Sikh wedding, and then a lengthy song and dance scene at the wedding itself, much in the character of Bollywood, with one or two Muslim guests being prominent.

There is a brief scene centred on a newspaper announcement of the imminence of the Partition in which Muslims express concern for their social cohesion with the Sikh community. The emphasis is then inverted as the camera focuses on a horde of impassioned Muslims, some bearing flaming torches, others menacingly brandishing swords and lathis, storming through the town. A very large group of armed and hostile Muslims try to break into the house of Bachchan Singh, Sukhmani's father, where a Muslim friend locks all the women safely in a room and then tries, unsuccessfully, to keep the door barred against the frenetic mob. There is then a longer than necessary fight scene in which Bachchan Singh and his Muslim friend take on the mob. Given the huge imbalance of numbers, the two friends ought to have been slaughtered within seconds, but the fight is protracted to show the heroism of the Muslim, who dies trying to save his Sikh friends against his own co-religionists, and the invincibility of Bachchan Singh who, seriously bruised and hacked, survives. The women are then brought out unharmed, though they can see that their future is dangerously precarious. Bachchan Singh is prevailed upon to 'give us our salvation'—such expressions as this and 'protect our honour' are euphemisms for 'kill us before the Muslims rape us'—and the old man is seen to feel that he has no other option. Here taste prevails over morbid sensationalism and the results of his appalling duty are shown briefly to inform that the duty has been done. Sad to say there is nothing exceptional in this awful 'moral' act, for there is abundant evidence in cinema and more in literature to establish the deaths of Sikh women at the hands of fathers, husbands and brothers, just as there is evidence of Sikh women committing suicide by jumping into wells. Sukhmani, however, survives her father's awful duty and we then see her as part of the refugee flight from what would soon become Pakistan to what would remain India.

It is all very dramatic, sometimes quite graphic and disturbing, but it is weakened by its presentation of the most significant aspects of the action as seemingly spontaneous and self-generating, while there is no attempt to account for the warm and profound Sikh–Muslim friendship suddenly turning into impassioned and vicious enmity. Indeed, making the home invasion so spectacular also makes it quite unrealistic and incredible, even amusing perhaps; consider, for instance, the sight of a bulky, middle-aged man leaping over staircases and throwing other men through the air while wielding a dagger with lethal effect. Here we have another example of the Partition being used as a vehicle for entertainment. Fortunately, the film improves somewhat when it gets to the events of 1984.

Gandhi poured scorn on the Old Testament notion of 'an eye for an eye and a tooth for a tooth', stating in Attenborough's film that it would be an effective way of making the whole world blind. Revenge is an assertion of brutishness and is self-propagating. Nevertheless, irrational and destructive as it may be, it is an emotion to which many do succumb from time to time. Indeed, we even hear of it being described as 'sweet'. The films discussed in this chapter unambiguously bear out the nature of vengeance as crude vendetta, especially its connection with human helplessness in a world that is changing rapidly beyond comprehension. Being suddenly uprooted, dispossessed and dislocated, all in a context of unrestrained violence and dire threats, is a nightmare to which nobody ever thinks they would be subjected. Sadly, the typical reaction to such a subjection is more often animal than rational.

Notes and References

1. A reference to the *Gita* and Lord Krishna's injunction to Arjuna, who is unwilling to wage war against his own kin, to do his duty as a Kshatriya and fight.

2. 'Hey Ram' is generally accepted to be Gandhi's last words as he faced his assassin.

3. For example, Suranjan Das, *Communal Riots in Bengal 1905–1947* (Oxford University Press, 1991); Nitish Sengupta, *Bengal Divided: The Unmaking of a Nation 1905–1971* (Viking, 2007); Debjani Sengupta, *The Partition of Bengal: Fragile Borders and New Identities* (Cambridge University Press, 2016).

six

In the Name of God

> 'Praise be to Allah, the Lord of the Universe.'
> 'Sat Sri Akal! Har Har Mahadev!'
> Spears flashed in the air and the old Mussalman's body was divided into four parts.
> The last name on the dying man's lips was God's, and on the lips of those who killed was God's Other name. And if there was an Almighty—somewhere far away, far above the killer and the killed—indeed He was a cruel tyrant.[1]

The Partition of India was an exercise in the re-arrangement of power, though it is so often seen as a division represented in religious terms. Put simply, the argument was that Hindus and Muslims were at each other's throats because they bore ineradicable differences from one another. Hindus wanted an undivided India, where they would be the majority; Muslims wanted a partition that would give them their own nation, Pakistan, where they would not have to live as a minority. The traps inherent in generalising are evident here. For example, the so-called ineradicable differences are not characteristic of the long history of Hindus and Muslims living together for centuries before the foreign conquest. Many Hindus were opposed to the idea of partition, although extremist bigots thought it was a good way to eliminate Muslims from the country; and while many Muslims were in favour of having their own Muslim homeland, considerably more elected to remain in India. Then there is a problem intrinsic to the terminology.

Hindu and *Muslim* are primarily religious terms; by extension they indicate communities, though in the broadest sense and with many variations accommodated by terms such as liberal, conservative, secular, extremist, progressive and so on. It is convenient to use simple, one-word labels, but they can mislead if we are not conscious of the variations inherent in them. Indeed, at the core of the controversy was *power*, not *religion*. This chapter examines films which foreground the endeavour to recruit and utilise God in the interests of earthly power.

The Partition of India was a political act, formalised by a foreign power urged to protect a perceived projection of its own national interests. Indeed, the Partition was urged by communal forces and opposed by secularists. Communalists would interpret it as a religious phenomenon, some seeing it as seeking a settlement to a religious disputation, others going so far as to call it a religious crusade. In India, communal definition is determined by religious affiliation, and not by ethnicity as in some other countries. However, like the European wars of religion some centuries ago, or the somewhat contemporaneous Irish dispute, the Partition had nothing to do with religious doctrine or theology or ritual; rather it had everything to do with the quest for power. It is often said that men do vile things in the name of religion, and in the struggle for power God can often be most grievously offended. Being exploited both for instigating malicious mischief and generating riots, religion emerges as the potential victim to be defended, even unto death, and there is much evidence of this being the case with the Partition of India. Truly horrible things were done to innocent and not so innocent people while loudly proclaiming the glory of Ishwar or Allah or Waheguru. In the name of their religion, men and women effectually turned their backs on God; in perpetrating evil deeds in His or Her name, they committed the most terrible blasphemies.

The two major communities have long taken issue with one another over relatively petty and peripheral matters. Noisy

Hindu festivities outside mosques or the Muslim abhorrence of pigs and Hindu protection of cows have been easily exploited by troublemakers intent on creating conflict. However, in a civilised society such divisive, anti-social behaviour is frowned upon and eclipsed by a general desire to live in harmony without having to appeal to religious sensibilities, still less to partition the country. The Sikh community, considerably less populous and concentrated mostly in Punjab and the north-western region of the country, is known for its militancy and the metaphors of bellicosity that colour its tradition; it is also noted and admired for its humanity and liberal-mindedness. However, while it does not tend to provocative offensiveness, its men are happy to be known as warriors of the Guru. Similarly, the two other major Indian religious communities maintain grounds fertile for conflict and a readiness to aggressively defend what they might consider to be righteousness. The importance of ritual and the prominence of bodily signification of identity keep the differences manifest; even the essentially private institution of male circumcision or its absence has damned to perdition or assured the salvation of many men caught up in the madness of communal violence. However, had the communal madness and intolerance of the later years of the colonial experience been characteristic of the thousand or so years of the pre-colonial history of the two, and later three, major communities living together, there would have been little but a wasteland for the foreigners to conquer and exploit. Religious difference does not presuppose dissension and conflict; it can equally demand and receive tolerance, mutual respect and peaceful co-existence.

It is often said that religion has done more to harm than to benefit mankind, that religion is known to bring out the worst in people. Religion, however, does not *do*; it simply *is*—it is adherents who are free to do or not do as they please. A number of Partition films represent some appalling inhumanity, much of it done in the name of God or religion. However, when people invoke the name of God in their quest to subjugate or to destroy others, when they claim that their killing is righteous, they are grossly and profoundly deluded. Those who assume a religious identity and use it to justify unimaginably irreligious and ungodly deeds are, in fact, abysmally ignorant of religion.

Dharmputra

While Yash Chopra's 1961 film, *Dharmputra* ('Adopted Son'), is realistic in its presentation, it has a strongly didactic intention. Thus the narrative, while always credible, is nevertheless concocted with a view to furthering the film's preceptive aim. While most of the other films discussed here take something of the historicity of the Partition as their basis or context, *Dharmputra* looks to the division of the country to develop and promulgate moral lessons. The morality may well be wholesome, but it is not necessarily aligned with actuality. Ultimately there remains a sense of contrivance given that the didactics and the actuality are at best associated rather than integrally connected.

The opening titles sequence helps set the tone. The titles are presented over the turning pages of a book containing sketches of the natural beauty of India, such as mountains and rivers, and of architectural splendour reflecting both Hindu and Muslim cultures. Heard over is a song extolling the excellence of India: 'Among all in the entire universe, our India is the best! ... the highest peak in the world, touching the skies, is our protector and guardian!'[2] The essential moral thrust is in the last line: 'Religion does not teach enmity between people! We are Indians, Hindustan is our country.'

The moral essence has been suggested and now the historical context is established. A title card telling us that it is 1925 is seen over a street march (the British flag flying on a building in the background reminds us of the unwanted foreign presence), the demonstrators crying for revolution and proclaiming the brotherhood of Hindus and Muslims. We might note that the dress and appearance of the participants is predominantly

Muslim and that all the placards are in Urdu script. We might also recall here that in 1925 the Muslim League had not yet been revitalised as a political force rivalling the Congress; that it was in the 1920s that Gandhi's work for Hindu–Muslim unity was launched; and that the deliberate feathering of the Muslim nest by the colonial power would not become evident and purposive for another 15 years or so. A voice-over asserts that the call for revolution is the call to freedom. We are told that Hindu and Muslim are not simply the names of two different communities but that they both stand for the

> one common culture of this country. Hindu and Muslim are the names of those two sons of this Motherland whose joys and sorrows, lives and deaths are joined together. Both of them have always been together, past, present and future. Hindus and Muslims are brothers and both are ready to die for their country.

Undoubtedly this is a fine nationalist sentiment, but one that is not argued for at any stage in the film; its affirmation at the beginning is simply to be accepted.

Then the narrative begins. Fundamental to it is the friendship between two now elderly men, Gulshan Rai and Nawab Badruddin, a Hindu and a Muslim, both rejoicing in a friendship which to them is more like a blood relationship. Gulshan dies, and the medical education of his son, Amrit, is taken care of by his 'uncle', the Nawab. At the beginning of the film, the old man comes to consult his 'nephew, more like a son,' on a painful, moral matter. His daughter, Bano, has fallen in love with a nondescript young man, Javed, and become pregnant. At first the Nawab forbids the notion of marriage between the two, given Javed's apparent lack of prospects. When he changes his mind, in sympathy with his daughter, the young man—as often happens in popular cinema—disappears without a trace. He will, of course, be rediscovered in circumstances of feasible improbability a little later in the film. Amrit suggests that they all go to the Nawab's villa in Shimla for the birth of the child, ensuring a degree of privacy away from Delhi, and it is there that he promulgates his solution to the moral threat posed by the advent of an illegitimate child. Babies being swapped at birth is hardly an unknown narrative device in Hindi cinema; here we have a variation of that—parents being swapped at birth. The communal integration, almost wholly accomplished by Gulshan and the Nawab, is thus consummated by the child of a Muslim man and woman being brought up as Dilip, the son and heir to Hindu parents, Amrit and his wife, Savitri. It does not, however, turn out to be a recipe for communal eugenics, for the boy grows up to be an obnoxious, anti-Muslim, Hindu extremist.

There is much mention, particularly in the songs and in the rhetoric of the older Dilip when he becomes a student leader in the nationalist cause, of dying for the Motherland, but ironically it is the aged Muslim Nawab who dies in defiant opposition to foreign rule, giving his blood for the cause of independent India, to which Dilip and his ilk will one day belong. The old man dies, crying out that Hindus and Muslims are brothers.

At this point it is convenient for the development of the narrative that Javed and Bano go abroad for 15 years, thus giving Dilip, who has now grown up and is studying law, ample time to completely forget that he ever knew them. A lot has happened in that time. We see a demonstration, visually much the same as the one at the beginning of the film, but the shouting and passion is no longer for Hindustan and for Hindu–Muslim unity, but for separatism and Pakistan.

The first shot we see of the mature Dilip is of him dressed only in a dhoti, his naked upper body revealing his sacred thread; he is sitting in a yogic posture, an open book of scripture before him, and an image of Saraswati, the goddess of learning and arts, to the side. There are other images and pictures around the room, including two of Vivekananda and one of the nationalist martyr, Bhagat Singh. Dilip's 'aunt', who has just returned from abroad, comes to meet him, and he goes to reverentially touch her feet but is struck by hearing the Muslim name Bano; he peremptorily completes the ritual greeting and angrily leaves the room. His 'mother', Savitri, is frank. 'Do you see how fanatic a Hindu he has turned out to be? He says Muslims shouldn't live here but should go back to where they came from.' (One might wonder how his 'parents' have allowed such an extreme position to develop but this is passed over.) Bano would comply with his wish, concerned only that the boy should lead a happy life, while Dilip proceeds to censure his sister and brothers for playing table tennis rather than attending to their morning prayers and rituals.

We learn from Savitri that Dilip has turned down several offers of marriage. Fundamental to his expectations of a wife is that she should be devoted to all the scripturally prescribed Hindu rituals and duties. Savitri tries to persuade him that one's thinking should keep up with the times, but the orthodox mind is not readily responsive to such reasoning. The anomalies of orthodoxy, such as widow burning, child marriage and the enslavement of women elicit only silence from him. There is one girl—Meena—with whom Savitri is quite taken, but Dilip will not even meet her on account of her having studied abroad for a couple of years. This prompts the formation of a conspiracy by Bano, one that serves the narrative only in fulfilling the need in popular cinema for a romantic element.

As we get closer to August 1947, the public mood is seen to be getting heated. We have had two demonstrations, one for freedom and Hindu–Muslim unity and one for partition. We now see a third, also for the soon-to-be independent nation. A group with placards in Hindi is marching for Hindu, Hindi, Hindustan; following close behind, carrying Pakistan flags and pro-Pakistan placards, is the rival group. Visually, this demonstration is presented in the same way as the previous two, except that in the previous two the demonstrators marched towards the camera and then turned out of the frame together; now the first group approaches the camera and goes out to the left of the frame, while the following group nears the camera and goes out to the right. It is a neat visual indication that the unity celebrated at the beginning of the film is now broken.

A speaker, not mentioned in the credits and looking rather like Jawaharlal Nehru, is addressing a huge gathering, declaring that the identity of a land is determined by its people, not by God. There is a cut to Dilip passionately asserting that the country must never be divided, for 'Bharat'[3] belongs to Hindus. If Muslims don't want to live with Hindus, they may go ... or we will compel them to go.' The man playing Nehru counters that India belongs to all those who consider it their nation, but that independence is paramount, and if independence can be achieved only with partition, then so be it. Dilip trots out all the tired old clichés that Muslims have always militated against Hinduism, spreading their own religion at the point of a sword, destroying thousands of temples and building mosques on the ruins, but 'they could never defeat the inner strength of the Hindu religion.' This is again countered by the assertion that so much blood has been shed in the name of religion, and given that millions of innocents have died, 'religion itself must be held culpable.'

The Partition is enacted and much of the rest of the film is set against the background of the physical expression of Dilip's subjective ranting. There is some very good presentation of rioting in the darkness, lit only by blazing torches. The visual effect of this in black and white is quite chilling. A voice-over tells us that 'the consequences of this division had never been heard or seen before in the history of humanity.' Here there are shots of buildings burning and mobs running rampant. 'Brothers became sworn enemies and the land was dyed with blood .... Someone committed an atrocity and someone else was punished.' There is a shot of Dilip rabble-rousing, warning that if the Ravi and Chenab rivers in Pakistan should flow with blood and corpses, then in India the banks of the mighty Ganges and Jamuna rivers will burst with uncountable dead bodies. It is, of course, all rhetoric, but very frightening nevertheless, especially coming from a highly educated young man of privileged upbringing. He gives the cry, 'Hail, Lord Hanuman!' and the crowd responds, 'Hail, Lord Shiva!' and proceeds to run wild.

There is an argument between Dilip and Amrit on the nature of religion. While Dilip stresses the outward observances such as rituals, Amrit insists that spiritual growth is essential. Dilip finds this hard to comprehend, and declares that Javed, injured in a riot and being treated in Amrit's house, is his enemy because he is Muslim. He also threatens his 'father' that if the patient stays, then he cannot live there. The audience must appreciate the grim irony in this, just as Amrit does, for the man Dilip declares to be his enemy is also, albeit unknown to him, his true father. With reason far more profound than Dilip can imagine, Amrit asserts, 'My house has no place for you.' By extension, the film is saying, 'Our nation has no place for communal bigots.'

Much of the passion for the Partition was irrational, stirred by utterly irrational people. Amrit's calm rationality only serves to enrage Dilip, and rather than respond to him rationally, he impulsively runs back to his rabble and makes another fervent speech about shedding blood for India, a rhetorical indulgence that ends with the chorus of 'Hail, Lord Hanuman! Hail, Lord Shiva!' In a state bordering on hysteria, Dilip returns to the house and directs his highly inflamed aggression at Amrit and Savitri. Amrit chides him for his arrogance and religious perversity, declaring him 'the enemy of goodness'. Reason has confronted passion and become passionate itself, for now comes the great moment of revelation when Dilip learns of his true biological identity, and is obliged to revise his beliefs about self and the nation however he will. In popular Indian cinema, the histrionic 'Better you had killed me at birth' will always seem fitting.

There is relief from what seems to be evolving melodrama. There is a disturbing sequence of file footage with a song playing over it. The singer, over shots of destruction and burning, laments that 'embers fly on the restless heart of the Motherland.' The song proceeds to question the point of this destruction and carnage, while the frame is filled with disturbing shots of unending trails of refugees and dead bodies, as havoc and desolation continue. The singer questions the worth of patriotism and pertinently wonders about the nature of God if blood is shed in His name. There is a shot showing the silhouette of women being abducted as the singer asks, 'What value will that religion hold if chastity is ruined in its name?' Ultimately, a simple fact is established: the excesses of the Partition cannot be justified or explained by reference to religious devotion; such cant only demeans religion. A little later the Nehru look-alike delivers a homily, rich in rhetoric but also sound in sentiment, asserting that religion does not preach enmity between people and blames vested interests for besmirching religion by planting hatred. Pledging fealty to the Motherland, he vows that only love will be the religion of India. It is sound sentiment indeed, but in the light of the fervour and turmoil of the time, more than a little naive.

Dilip, bemoaning his newfound identity, wallows for a time in self-pity. It is all egoism, with no mention of service for nation-building or uplift of the poor. Dilip, the revered leader, has through no action of his own spontaneously become a traitor who must be killed. The passions of the Partition notwithstanding, there is little realism in this. However, the point is to establish the ease with which the notions of culpability, enmity and righteous aggression might flourish, fade or become contorted.

In terms of realism it is hard to imagine how this film could end happily, but it is Hindi commercial cinema after all, and the end is indeed happy. There is an angry mob seething outside the house. Dilip stands before them defiantly, flanked by his two 'mothers', ready to atone for his actions. But then the police—and Meena—come to the rescue. The former saves him from the mob, while Meena gives him his new identity, leading him to declare, 'We will create a new world … where only humanity will be worshipped.' We might ignore the fact that only five minutes ago Dilip could not have dreamt of mouthing these words or rejoicing with his mixed 'family' on the bridge between the two houses, representing the bridge between Hindus and Muslims in India. The tricolour is raised, the cry goes up, 'We are Hindi. Hindustan is our country!', and there is a reprise of the opening song, 'Among all in the entire universe, our India is the best!'

Dharmputra is unashamedly didactic cinema. Its realism is plausibly—and commendably—contrived to create a moral lesson on melding communal differences into nationalism. Given this underlying artificiality, along with the conventional devices of the post-natal interchange, the steadfast strength of mother images, and the power of one who will surely become a mother, it is quite remarkable that the film's didactic intent survives its genuine cogency. What may unavoidably appear as naive is not necessarily to be spurned; perhaps a touch of naiveté is essential to all idealism.

Tamas revisited

A notably different kind of film is Govind Nihalani's *Tamas*, which was introduced in Chapter 5. In this superb cinematic epic, Nihalani takes great pains to present an experience of the Partition that is both comprehensive and balanced. The simple binary of 'Hindu–Muslim' that colours the conflict in many films on the Partition is inadequate to his purpose, and so here we see a substantial focus given to the Sikhs and to a sect probably largely unknown outside of India, the Rababis. Nihalani is also careful to balance this with the secular alternative to religion represented by the Indian National Congress as well as by those aligned much further to the political left.

The Partition's Hindu–Muslim binary is often seen, not entirely correctly, in political terms as represented by the Congress on the one hand and the Muslim League on the other. However, Jinnah consistently tried the patience of Congress leaders with his insistence that the Congress was a Hindu party, for whom independence meant the establishment of a Hindu Raj. The challenge of the counterclaim—that there were, and always had been, Muslims in the general membership of the Congress as well as in its leadership—was met by the denigration of such Muslims for their alleged infidelity to Islam. Jinnah never tried to conceal his contempt, for example, for the staunch nationalist leader of the Congress and eminent Muslim, Maulana Abul Kalam Azad. Of course, the majority of Congress members were Hindus, but then so were the majority of the country's population. Rather than trying to minimise the worth of the Congress—a declared secular political party—by claiming that it was not secular, closer to the truth would be the claim that the Muslim League, like the Hindu Mahasabha, was a manifestly communal organisation.

In *Tamas* the initial confrontation between these two major groups shows the endeavour of the League members to paint the Congress in communal terms and the attempt by the Congressmen to assert their secularity. There is an interesting shot—taken from inside a dargah, looking out on to a street—of the Congressmen preparing to do social service by cleaning public sewage gutters. Just before the conclusion of the shot, a Muslim man is seen coming to make obeisance at the shrine and it is evident that he and the Congressmen just outside are quite unaware of one another. The elements of this shot might be interpreted as associating the League with religion and the Congress with secular public service.

We then come to the initial fallout from the provocative insult intended by the dumping of the dead pig in front of the mosque. What the greater scheme of the sacrilege might have been we are not told; it could have been political, religious spite or even mere mischief. All that matters is that as provocation it worked. The immediate response is a retaliatory outrage towards the Other religion with the killing of a cow, and the traditional religious battle lines are drawn. There is no point in trying to deal rationally with anti-social recklessness; 'God' has been offended and there is no honour in sitting on your hands.

The Hindu warriors in the looming battle are presented to us and they are not members of the local branch of the Congress. After a short segment showing the end of a Hindu ritual, there is a meeting of the inner circle—probably the leaders of the Hindu Mahasabha and connections to the RSS—in a room behind the temple. There is talk of storing oil for boiling and using it as a weapon along with burning coals—primitive indeed, but establishing at least the suggestion of a link with the epic past. There is a demand to activate the Yuvak Samaj or the 'youth group' and to provide them with lathi training and martial arts skills in order to defend Hinduism, all with a liberal dose of religious discourse and the offering of venerations to a fire. As Ranbir walks through the street with his guru, Devrath, he is told, 'Remember, Ranbir, we have to establish a Hindu state, and it is necessary to destroy our enemy for it.' We have seen how Ranbir was obliged to prove his manly worth as a warrior for Hinduism by slaughtering a chicken, and how that test filled him with the 'heroism' needed to sneak up behind an old Muslim man in the street and senselessly stab him to death. This whole Hindu Mahasabha section is an excellent illustration of the conflation of mythology and religion to cultivate politically-motivated violence, a programme quite non-existent in the Congress' platform.

And yet, a little later, when Jarnail Singh—the passionate Sikh loyalist of the Congress—rides through the streets in a carriage, crying out through a megaphone about the brave warriors who will destroy the enemies of India, we may be a little disturbed at the similarity in rhetoric between the secular and the religious. Nevertheless, the secular does remain secular, and as we saw earlier, it is upheld by the Congress and bolstered by the Communists. However, the fires of the night are fanned by fanatics—or simpletons—crying out religious slogans as though that might justify the dreadful deeds they were perpetrating. The cries of 'Hail, Lord Mahadev!' outside the house of the humble Muslim schoolteacher, Karimdin, are for a moment quite blood-curdling; there is an amazing sense of relief when he is rescued by his neighbour, a Sikh woman who defies her own menfolk to deliver him to safety. But then one war cry to God is answered by another; at the cry of 'Praise to Allah! Allah is great', the Muslim men on the lower level of Lala's house promise to protect him. If the audience is not cynical by now, it soon will be when the Muslim Shahnawaz callously and without cause kills the disabled Hindu houseboy, Nanku, purely on the basis of religious difference.

The focus shifts to the Sikh community. Inside a gurudwara, Sikh men, women and children are gathered while outside there are developing threats of Muslim militancy. Again, it would seem, a gauntlet will be picked up, no matter who might have thrown it down, if indeed it was thrown down at all. The leader of the gurudwara offers a prayer invoking the names of the Sikh Gurus, beseeching God to grant them victory, courage and divine blessing. The piety of the faith that proclaims 'victory to those who recite the name of God with a true heart' might seem evident, but *victory* presupposes *defeat*, and the most common means of defeat is the weaponry of destruction and death. There is a cut to the outside and the shouts of 'Allah is great!' remind us that this eddy of piety is being stirred with a view to incite violent conflict.

We learn that the voice of reason, that of a young Sikh with connections to the Communist boys whom we met earlier, has been used to try to dispel the friction between the two communities which, it is asserted, is being deliberately instigated by outsiders. The leader of the gurudwara pleads that he too has tried to reach out to the Muslim leadership but they are not to be trusted. Clichéd suspicion and misgiving are also employed as bastions of argument by the Muslim side. Dilawar, the Muslim butcher, asserts the blatant perfidy of the Sikhs in 'now storing up arms' in their temple. However, the notion of cohesion between the Muslim and Sikh communities is given voice by the Rababis, a group of Muslim singers who have been singing hymns of the Guru for generations. Their leader bemoans the fact that today they may not enter the gurudwara and, if they sing the hymns at home, they will be branded as infidels. From now on the voices of reason and cohesion will be drowned out by those of fanaticism, belligerently calling on their God. These cries are heard over close shots of the Sikh congregation, of Mirza and Meerdad, of the Rababis, and of the Muslim butcher, Dilawar.

As night falls, flaming torches light up the smoke-screened scenes of the day's destruction. The Rababi's prayer, one of the very few truly religious expressions in Partition cinema, invokes the divine but is moved by compassion in a very ordinary, human way.

> Truly my Lord, have mercy. What kind of destruction is this? Why has the cheerful village under your care turned into a cemetery? My Allah, the omniscient, benevolent, peace be upon Allah Rakaah who left the village to fetch water for Sheikh Gulam Rasul and himself became a victim to the Sheikh's gun. Peace be upon old Saudagar Singh, whose family forgot to take him to the gurudwara. Forgive the poor unknown fellow who lost his life in the skirmish of the battle. Take care of the children who worked for Fateh Din and used to play there innocently but became victims of this bloodshed. My God! *Mere Sat Guru* [there is a cut to a portrait of the guru to whom Mir is praying], shield all those innocent people who became victims of this blind religious war and are now at your doorstep. Have mercy. Have mercy, my Lord.

In this case, God, who is addressed as Allah, is visually represented by the icon of a Sikh guru. The inter-faith fusion here, or what Christians would call ecumenism, is telling in its simplicity. Even more telling is the fact that most people chose to remain distant from it.

While people are so audacious as to invoke the name of God while doing abominable things to one another, arrogantly assuming that whatever is done in the name of God must be pleasing to the divine, the Rababi elicits faith in a God who cares about the sufferings of people rather than the causes they espouse. The Rababi's sense of the divine immanent in the human suggests a contrast to the mindless sloganeering of the mob. Those whose religiosity extends not much further than catchcries and formalised rituals are guilty of blasphemy rather than of being virtuous in their glorification of God. So many people seen in *Tamas* and in other films are unthinking and easily led, taking on the appurtenances of religion for motivation and inspiration in a cause that is by no means religious. The same appurtenances are also assumed to justify or even make righteous the wickedness perpetrated 'in defence of religion'.

Khamosh Pani revisited

The demand for Pakistan as a specifically Muslim homeland carved out of India would inevitably determine a partition process that expressed itself in many ways as a communal conflict. Despite the vociferously proclaimed secularism of the Congress, so many of its followers and would-be followers became ardently partisan in the face of the Other's claims on their land and ancestral property. Some screamed fealty to Mahadev or Ma Kali and others to Waheguru, to match the separatists' cries proclaiming the greatness of Allah. Nationalism had been conflated with religion. As a postscript to this discussion on films dealing with the religious decking of emerging nationalisms, we will look again at *Khamosh Pani*, a film dealt with in Chapter 4.

Here the narrative basis for the articulation of nationalism enveloped in religion is the coming to the small town, in which the film is set, of two young men, Mazhar and Rashid—devout Muslims, militant Islamicists and right-wing activists. They meet up with Salim, the young and innocent boy who dreams of marrying his beloved Zubeida, and they gradually seduce him to their cause. The cause is very close to fanaticism and apparently has the political purpose of exploiting Islam as a national religion—or state ideology—to entrench, we may assume, the power of General Zia-ul-Haq, devout servant of God and power-hungry military dictator. In the interests of consolidating state power, religion is reinterpreted to be a force for national unity, which is really a euphemism for exclusivity. It is intolerant of Others and, indeed, inimical to them. It even lays stress on blood authenticity, calling into doubt, at least temporarily, Salim's credentials as a genuine Muslim given the fact that Ayesha, his mother, was born a Sikh and later converted to Islam. Whether it is out of love for her son or an inability to live within the constraints of zealotry, Ayesha commits suicide like her female relatives had done a generation ago.

That Sharia nationalism is something to be fostered rather than an already existent public state of mind is suggested at a teashop by a barber, who questions the authenticity of the words of Zia-ul-Haq, pointing out that the political class and the common man speak with different voices. Later one of the activists says that strict adherence to Islam is the will of the Almighty, provoking from the barber a contemptuous retort about being told what to think by 'kids like you'.

Rashid tells Salim's friend that faith is basic to the nation and that praying five times a day is the way to invigorate that faith. It is with the allusion to the Russian preparation for the invasion of Afghanistan (1980) that we might assume nationalism and, indeed, Islam will emerge in a new light. Being an unemployed young man with no evident prospects, Salim is easily drawn into this mix of faith and nascent chauvinism. He goes with Mazhar and Rashid to a function outside of town and on the way, on the back of a truck, they excite themselves and each other with the frenetic shouting of slogans and raising fists to the heavens.

A little later we see them enter a hall where the speaker is giving a clear example of an endeavour to fuse nationalism with religion. He tells his audience of the faithful that fasting is a means to the forgiveness of sins and prayer is a key to heaven. The link between such religious experience and state chauvinism would seem to be in the next notion on his agenda: *jihad*.[4] He tells his audience that the man who performs jihad is not tainted by greed or fear, and then he challenges his audience, asking if the Almighty has bestowed on them this great gift of righteous striving. There is a spontaneous and fervid response, 'Our resolve is jihad!' along with an equally fervid bout of sloganeering. The speaker then reminds them of the attainment in 1947 of independence, not of Pakistan, but of 'this nation in the name of Islam'. The nation was gained with 'the blood of our Muslim brothers', yet after 30 odd years it has been soured by the corruption of politicians. This is probably an allusion to the deposing, trial and hanging of Zulfikar Ali Bhutto by General Zia, a Muslim soldier and not a Westernised, secular politician. Then he concludes with another challenge: 'And if you understand the meaning of Islam, come forward and show them all! Whoever dies in the holy war shall certainly have their way in Heaven!' This is answered by loud cries of 'Long live Pakistan!' Here there is a simple slide from fasting and prayer to killing in righteous conflict—a neat conflation of nationalism and religion. It might also remind us of the bellicose quasi-religious rhetoric of Dilip in *Dharmputra*.

The exclusive nature of state religion throws up another dichotomy in public behaviour. Under a recent agreement between the governments of India and Pakistan, Sikhs are given the freedom to visit their holy places in the country that they and their forebears were obliged to leave three decades ago. Thousands of Sikh visitors are seen descending upon the town and as they throng the narrow streets, a number of locals—such as the barber from the teashop—offer them a cordial and respectful welcome. This contrasts with the attitude of the two activists and Salim on a rooftop overlooking the street below; they delight in crude humour about the Sikhs and their appearance. Quite often, of course, what germinates as a joke mushrooms into something grim, and soon the unschooled boys' unpleasantness becomes frankly hostile and culminates in a menacing confrontation with Sikh elders in which the visitors are told plainly to go away. In other words, Muslims should not have to tolerate the actuality of an Other. The activists march off, shouting their righteous slogans and glorying in their God and His Prophet.

The young innocent Salim is at the forefront of this hostility, having developed rapidly into an angry bully. As a staunch supporter of radical Islam, he has become quite dislikeable. The fulfilment of his transformation is seen in the last minutes of the film when he appears on the screens of television sets on display in a retail store. There is an easy message in the multiplicity of sets being ignored by the many passers by. Zubeida, now a mature and modern woman, watches with a hint of bemusement a man identified by a TV screen title as 'Saleem Khan, Seceratary' (*sic*) of some Islamic society. He now has a full beard, is soft-spoken, and by all appearances lost to the cause. Zubeida smiles and walks away from him to get on with her life.

While in the 1940s Jinnah's demand for Pakistan was indeed a radical one and inspired many outpourings of religious fervour, it hardly anticipated the melding of political power and the military and later, the conflation of state ideology and religion. Nevertheless, the Two Nation Theory, inadvertently perhaps, allowed for the possibility of the new nation going in that direction. Apart from what goes on in the memory of Ayesha, all of *Khamosh Pani* takes place more than 30 years after new lines were drawn on the map, yet it is all so very firmly rooted in that revision of political geography.

Pakistan could be an economic and social success without an exclusive official state religion; Islam can continue to be a noble and beautiful religion without being politicised to enhance the ambitions of power-hungry men. What really is needed is a policy to curb the influence of men who would act as God's deputies.

In the context of Indian history, *religion* has an elasticity of meaning. It may imply theology, scriptural doctrine and ritual, or it may imply a community. In most of the films discussed in this book, it is intended in the latter sense but very often with a tinge, though less than meagre, of the former usage. *Dharmputra* tries to go beyond this meagreness, and to some extent it is successful, such as in Dilip's references to Hindu tradition, *shastric* duty and the like. Nevertheless, the references are little more than mentions. When he is challenged regarding some of them, he remains silent and nothing is established or obviated. The didactic intent of the film is to enhance the view that religion—in any sense—should never be used to divide people and that true nationalism is built on the unity of all. While it is a sound belief, it leaves the nature of religion in the context of the Partition largely unexplained. *Tamas*, on the other hand, exposes the violence of Partition as an expression of mindless fanaticism, allowing its assumed religiosity no credence at all. The infernal flames blazing against the dark night sky are a telling reminder that religion, the bringing of order out of chaos, is absent here and now. Moreover, in addition to negating the hollow righteousness of those who would go to war in defence of a God, Govind Nihalani offers a positive expression in the form of a Rababi prayer in opposition to the politicised misuse of religion. *Khamosh Pani*, with its roots set deep in the Partition, warns us quite plainly of the viciousness and the intellectual, moral and cultural aridness if religion and politics—or religion and nation—were in one way or another to become fused, albeit 30 years later. All three films do have one idea in common, and that is the belief that religion is debased when it is flaunted by people who are unworthy and largely ignorant of it.

Notes and References

1. Krishan Chander, *Traitor*, translated from *Ghaddaar* (1960) by Rakhshanda Jalil (New Delhi: Westland, Tranquebar Press, 2017), p. 80.
2. The highest peak in the world is Mt Everest, across the summit of which runs the border of Nepal and China.
3. The ancient (pre-Muslim) name for India.
4. A righteous struggle, which may be against an enemy of Islam or against the power of sin within the individual.

seven

Home is Where the Heart is

Like a huge natural disaster, not anticipated until it was too late to be avoided, the Partition hit India with devastating effect. So many things of an unprecedented nature suddenly had to be attended to: relief had to be provided for so many of the dispossessed who had suffered the wounds of conflict, contracted disease, or experienced starvation and become malnourished; efforts had to be made to reunite fractured families and to repatriate abducted women; relief accommodation had to be set up for the untold numbers of refugees, all of whom were homeless and most of them jobless; and two national economies had to be built on the foundations of weakened infrastructure and depleted popular morale. These tasks and others like them were indeed mammoth, yet they also carried a sense of urgency. However, given their magnitude and the long delay in producing results, despair and hopelessness might readily set in. Probably there were those who were realistic enough to accept fate as it had been handed to them, and with mustered or even conjured optimism, embarked on a new chapter in their lives. For many, though, the heartsickness engendered by the dejection brought about by wretchedness and misery could just as easily take the form of a profound nostalgia in which the longing for what was irretrievably lost might lead to unbearably painful suffering.

Four films of Ritwik Ghatak

The Bengali filmmaker, Ritwik Ghatak, was born in Dacca[1] in what was then East Bengal, and moved with his family to West Bengal a little ahead of the migratory waves impelled by the Famine of 1943 and the Partition four years later. He had, therefore, some understanding of displacement, separation and loss. While it cannot be said that any of his eight feature films is actually *about* the Partition, the experience of dislocation and deprivation thrown up by it is integral to most of his work.

Ghatak's first film, *Nagarik* ('The Citizen', 1952[2]), describes the plight of an East Bengali refugee family living in extremely straitened conditions in Calcutta. A calendar on the wall displays a picture of an attractive house in a pleasant environment, a motif perhaps of something to look forward to eventually, or of what has in fact been lost forever. The family survives on the meagre pension of the ageing father while hoping for better days when the son, Ramu, a graduate, will get the good job that thousands of similarly well-educated young men are also seeking.

The dislocation being endured here is more temporal than geographic. There is no evidence that things are any better in what is now East Pakistan, and in fact India would struggle for decades to rebuild an economy ruined by centuries of oppressive and exploitative imperialist rule. Nevertheless, while there is yearning for the past, the immediate understanding of the misery of the present is to be discerned in the actuality of displacement. In other words, while the yearning is, in fact, temporal, it is interpreted as spatial and geographical. The Partition, anonymous and not even referred to, hovers like a grim shadow defining the film's atmospherics.

Meghe Dhaka Tara ('The Cloud-Capped Star', 1960) has as its focus a similar family who have been living for some 10 years in what the mother sees as imposed hardship. Here the subjective significance of the calendar picture in *Nagarik* is conveyed by a framed photograph of the family's two older children, Shankar and Nita, in another place at a much earlier time, indicating that the yearning is again temporal as well as geographical. The references to hills and fresh air are, like the pretty house in the calendar, indicative of both nostalgia and a dream of the future.

The family is educated middle-class, known in Bengal as *bhadralok*, and it is suggested that the social consequences of a decline in economic circumstances is harder for them than for others. Small details underline their dire straits: a close-up of Sanat's shirt reveals a fray at the shoulder seam, while a similar shot of Shankar's shirt shows a right-angle tear; Nita's breaking her sandal on the rough surface of the road erupts as a major problem as it will cost money to have the sandal fixed; and a major boon in Shankar's life is the acquisition of a razor blade. The family of six, in rented accommodation, get by on the father's wages as a schoolmaster and on the fees taken as a tutor of private students by Nita, herself an M.A. student. But when the father has an accidental fall, after which he can barely walk, all responsibility falls on Nita. Such hardship makes it difficult for the family to maintain its middle-class appearances, and when Mantu fails in college and takes up a job at a factory, the father is aghast. Then the boy suffers a serious accident at the factory and money has to be found for his hospital bills. Nita is moved to observe, 'Childhood seems so far away, and those hills don't seem to be of this earth.'

While in *Nagarik* and *Meghe Dhaka Tara*, thoughts provoked by the Partition enrich the background to the narrative, in Ghatak's next film, *Komal Gandhar* (1961), they are given a more focal significance. The title literally means the musical note 'E flat' and carries some suggestion of harmony within tension. Although the uncharacteristically happy ending might suggest the triumph of harmony, disharmony is prominent throughout much of the film, and it is here that we might find the significance of the Partition. Central to the narrative is a theatre company which has had a 'partition' of its own, and now become two rival companies. In an attempt at reconciliation the two groups come together to mount a production of the classic, *Shakuntala,* but the endeavour is doomed to fail. There is lingering friction within the company as well as internal dissension within individuals, all of which militates against a united endeavour and shared achievement.

Komal Gandhar opens with the performance that had led to the split of the theatre company. An old man is being persuaded to leave his home beside the Padma river and become a refugee. On a screen set up as a backdrop we see silhouettes of people moving from the right side to the left—or across the border—to make a new life somewhere else. The old man laments that he is leaving his mother, for here he had performed her last rites; there is also the poetic suggestion of one's homeland as mother. In the last act of the play, the party has reached Calcutta, and a woman is distressed that her husband, who has taken their younger son with him to fetch water, has not returned. Here we might recall some scenes from *Chinnamul* of the ocean of people in that vast metropolis and the frightening reality of becoming lost in the unknown.

The theatre troupe makes a visit to the Padma, and while most of them amuse themselves in a boat race which has no apparent narrative significance, the focus is on Anusua, who has returned from the breakaway group, and Bhrigu, the leader of the troupe. As they sit beside the river, looking across to what is now East Pakistan, Anusua expresses a sense of nostalgia at being so close to what was once her home. Bhrigu, too, remembers his home on the other side. They are at the dead end of a railway track, truncated by the river, and he remembers getting down there after visits to Calcutta, and his mother waiting for him. 'I thought that the rail track was a joining point, but now it has become a dividing place.' There is reminiscence of the pleasures they had in childhood and then Bhrigu recalls how it all ended so grimly: 'Father died like a beggar and mother almost died starving.' Bhrigu traces his own loneliness to this sad turnaround. The point of the separation is made in a shot which looks as though taken from the front of a train running away from the camera along the railway line toward the river; the movement continues through the dead end, not into the river but into darkness, suggesting loss, confusion, maybe even death. The film ends on a note of optimism, reflected in a troupe member, Kunal, writing a play about the Partition of Bengal, and in Anusua and Bhrigu's shared enthusiasm for the work.

Komal Gandhar is a clear statement of preference for harmony over disharmony. Bickering and backbiting might give some passing petty satisfaction but the worth of that satisfaction is nullified by the destructiveness of the good that might have made it greater and more lasting. Sabotage of a performance from within is a contradiction of art itself. By extension, whatever satisfaction might have been gained by the minimisation of a homeland is also transitory, as is indicated by the continuing yearnings for the life that was on the other side of the river.

In *Subarnarekha* (1962[3]), the Partition is perceived as something of an umbrella covering a number of separations that form the narrative of the film. The umbrella is established right at the start, with the opening shot of the raising of the Indian flag in a makeshift school in a refugee colony in Calcutta. The school is run by two friends, Ishwar and Haraprasad; the latter is married, has children and is a hopeless idealist, while Ishwar is a bachelor looking after his much younger sister, Sita. The first significant separation of the film is that of a little boy, Abhiram, from his widowed mother; Ishwar is magnanimous and takes the little boy with him, intending to bring him up as Sita's brother. By chance he meets up with Ram Vilas, a Marwari friend from former times who is now a highly successful businessman, who offers him a job with accommodation in Chhatimpur, outside of Calcutta and beside the Subarnarekha river. Given his responsibility for two small children, it is an offer Ishwar can hardly refuse. Haraprasad scorns him as a deserter, and so another separation is effected. Abhiram yearns for his mother, which many in the audience might easily conflate with *desh*—'country' or 'home'—while Sita yearns for the home she does not remember ever having. So, with the move to Chhatimpur, a period of happiness begins, despite the separations that had to be endured.

After a time we learn that Haraprasad has failed to make a new life for himself and his family; he has lost jobs in seven schools and has been reduced to begging. In despair, his wife hangs herself and gradually Haraprasad loses his mind. After suffering displacement in his flight from East Bengal, he has come to see himself as a misfit, unable to belong anywhere. The happiness of Ishwar and the two children, now approaching adulthood, also starts to fray and a sad process of decline sets in. Under the influence of the orthodox Ram Vilas, Ishwar tries to distance himself and Sita from Abhiram, whom Ram Vilas fears might be of low caste (as it turns out, he is); he also tries to arrange a suitable marriage for Sita—one that would meet with the approval of Ram Vilas.

The last part of the film shows a descent into utter degradation. The tragic sequence of events follows the elopement of Sita and Abhiram. Abhiram, an honours graduate and recently trained bus driver, accidentally runs over and kills a little girl and is beaten to death by an irate mob. Ishwar and Haraprasad fall into moral abandon, exposed in a scene in a Western style nightclub complete with European dress, party hats, plastic whistles and foreign dance music, where in such inanity they patently do not fit. Later Ishwar is persuaded to visit a singing girl, who turns out to be Sita. Overwhelmed by shame, thinking that he has come to her for sex, Sita kills herself. All Ishwar has left now is his little nephew, Binu, the orphan son of Sita and Abhiram, whose union he had strenuously opposed.

Put in such summary form, it all sounds like an elaborate piece of melodrama. What makes it so intensely sad, however, is the simple credibility by which one aspect of the nightmare moves on to the next. Perhaps a key to its meaning may be found in the nightclub where Haraprasad, who was the worse for drink, falls off his chair and the waiter asks Ishwar to take his friend home. Ishwar is bemused. 'Home?' he asks, as though, given the circumstances, that is the silliest word that could possibly have been uttered. Through almost all of their adult lives they have been the unwitting playthings of displacement—settling nowhere, belonging nowhere, fitting in nowhere. Ishwar wants to raise the question of blame, as though the acknowledgement of culpability might help make sense of the whole nightmare, but there are no simple answers. Certainly their first major displacement set the downward spiral in motion and the wholesale displacements on either side of the country were directly caused by the Partition. However, someone seeking solace in rationality would find little comfort in such an explanation.

The film ends with hope, for Uncle will take Binu to his new home, the one he has heard about from his mother. The final shots follow the man and the little boy as they walk along the riverbank, away from the camera towards what might meaningfully be described as 'home'. Even in these final shots Ishwar is still a refugee, but now he is no longer in despair as he is being led by a symbol of optimism and hope.

The straitened circumstances of the *bhadralok* family in *Nagarik*, the poverty, accidents and illness in *Meghe Dhaka Tara*, the bitchy dissensions in *Komal Gandhar*, and Ishwar's misery and Haraprasad's failings in *Subarnarekha* are all part of the fallout of the Partition. Other aspects of that fallout might well have been the destinies of some who, through a stroke of good fortune, landed on their feet at the end of the migratory journey and never looked back. Of course, they would have been fewer in number, but the point still stands that deprivation and provision, or misery and happiness, cannot come unmodified from the same cause.

Ghatak only comes close—and that too, rarely—to confronting the Partition as a historical actuality. Rather, his representations of it are indirect and usually seen as symptoms. To him, and probably to the majority of his viewers, it is a worthy enough achievement to adequately depict the multifarious sufferings of ordinary, innocent people and to create in his audience depths of pity that might generate true and meaningful compassion. It is here that Ghatak's value as an interpreter of the Partition lies.

Shankhachil revisited

A personal yearning for a life that has for ever been lost can be clearly represented in narratives in which individuals offer their own stories. The films of Ritwik Ghatak do this exceptionally well and, indeed, most movingly. In other films there is an acknowledgement, tacit or manifest, of a larger socio-cultural context which, despite the upheavals, remained largely unpartitioned. The partition in the east was experienced prominently as the Partition of Bengal. A number of films clearly suggest that while a line was drawn on the map, separate governments and administrative systems instituted, and large communally-determined population shifts occurred, *Bengaliness*, although threatened, was not destroyed. There were indeed communal riots in the east to demonstrate exceptions to the rule, but the rule was and seems to have remained that, culturally at least, Bengalis are Bengalis first and Hindus or Muslims second. It would be starry-eyed to suggest that Bengaliness obviates communalism, but it is quite reasonable to argue that communalism has been held in check, at least to some extent, by the strength and depth of a common culture.

The appeal of that common culture is eloquently spoken for in Goutam Ghose's *Shankhachil*. The film was introduced in Chapter 2 to illustrate a humanitarian anomaly in the institution of the border and its implications, while in this chapter it is looked at from the point of view of cultural identity. In considering the essence of 'partition' and 'border' it would be unrealistic to confine our thoughts to geographical and socio-political data. With such data a clerk can determine someone's national identity, but he cannot assess the value of that identity for that individual without also considering its substantial cultural substratum. We are who we are largely due to the non-material gifts that we inherit: myths and stories, songs and poems, rituals and festivals—the things that define an ethos. Undivided Bengal was very rich in such things and in 1947, many Bengalis feared that along with the division of the land there would also be a division of an ethos. The two parts of it might have been described as Hindu and Muslim, but Bengalis had never been inclined to define themselves culturally by resorting to religious nomenclature. As far as cultural identity was concerned, they saw themselves primarily as Bengali, and other terms such as 'Muslim' and 'Hindu' were ancillary to this. The tragedy in Goutam Ghose's film is that a little girl dies, and her devoted parents are at least shown the inside of an Indian jail because the border presupposes protocols that give prominence to one's bureaucratic manageability, while any human values that would normally arise out of a common cultural identity are simply unacknowledged. Much of the first half of the film is devoted to a depiction of the significant cultural inheritance of the Bengalis in the life of a humble Bangladeshi schoolteacher, Badal.

There is an allusion to this shared cultural inheritance as early as the opening titles, where the credit for the songs heard in the film is given to Rabindranath Tagore, Kazi Nazrul Islam, Jibanananda Das and Rajanikanta Sen. Three of these four were Hindus, and we soon learn that the film's spatial focus is Bangladesh—former East Pakistan. It is a simple indication that the songs are Bengali and that the labels 'Hindu' and 'Muslim' are not relevant. Soon after we meet Badal, the father of the little girl, Rupsha, there is a reference to the philosophy of history of the great writer, Bibhutibhushan Bandyopadhyay, another Hindu, and it is the history of the common people, not of kings and empires.

We see Badal in the classroom preparing his students for the following day's celebration of International Mother Language Day. Bengalis on both sides of the border have long been inordinately proud of their language. Badal reminds his students of the passionately commemorated language movement in East Pakistan in protest against Jinnah's determination that Urdu should be the one and only official language of the new nation, and that martyrs arose out of the fervour of that movement. Himself a Muslim, he tells them that they are Bengali first and then Muslim, and that their identity is determined by their language, which 'has no religion.' He starts singing a song, which is carried over into the scene of the next day's celebrations, a song which praises the Bengali language and refers (with what some might see as ecumenical audacity) to the Mother Goddess, while exhorting the advance of Bengal's children, both Hindu and Muslim. We might note the absence of Two Nation Theory thinking here.

A sense of one Bengal, despite the border, simmers throughout the film. There is a lovely scene in which Badal and Rupsha are sitting beside the vast river at dusk. Pointing to a flock of birds flying on high, Badal tells his little girl that they are flying to India and then they will return to Bangladesh. Her simple question in response is, 'Then why can't we?' She goes on to ask about the tigers of the Sundarban[4] and the crocodiles, seeking to know which are Indian and which are Bangladeshi. Badal jokes that the tigers and the crocodiles 'have eaten up the map itself' and concludes wistfully, 'If only men could eat up borders.'

Although set more or less contemporaneously, *Shankhachil* makes one telling and substantial reference to 1947. While doing some research for an article he wants to write, Badal looks into some old family letters in a case thick with dust and crawling with cockroaches. One letter, which he starts to read, was probably written to his father, and the writer expresses concern about the communal riots that are driving Hindus from East

Bengal into India. He speaks of a Hindu family he had sheltered in his home for a few days, during which time thugs looted their house and took possession of it. They even urinated on the holy basil tree and danced over their work of destruction. 'As a pious Muslim, witnessing this humiliation of another's religion has left me ... ashamed, and I realised that rioters have no religion. They are worshippers of the sect called hatred.' The writer sadly concludes that the identity tags of 'Hindu' and 'Muslim' have replaced the Bengali identity. Some 70 years later, Badal and his schoolchildren would suggest that this is not entirely true, although at the end of the film, at Rupsha's funeral, blame for her death is readily apportioned to the Hindu headmaster, who is told: 'It's all your fault, devoted Indian. Why don't you go and live *there* [in India]?' Yet this hint of communal bigotry might suggest more about the letter writer's thugs than men of minds like Badal's.

From the beginning of the film to the end, the river is seen as an image of the defiance of borders and an emblem of Bengaliness. 'O river, to whom do you belong? To Muslims or Hindus?' The frequent shots of birds also represent a condition unconfined and undefined by borders, as suggested by the film's title and its English substitute, 'Boundless'. As the film draws to a close there is a shot of a *shankhachil* on a tree outside Badal's house, a poignant moment that conjures up memories of a little girl's delight in the vast, un-partitioned world of Nature. From the shankhachil, the camera focuses for a time on the barbed wire border, and then, most pointedly, on a flock of birds flying over it.

Chitra Nadir Pare

A story of challenged identity is told by the Bangladeshi filmmaker, Tanvir Mokammel. *Chitra Nadir Pare* ('Quiet Flows the River Chitra', 1998) is set in Narail, a provincial town on the banks of the Chitra river in the newly created East Pakistan.

Its focus is on Shashikanta Sengupta, a Hindu lawyer in the predominantly Muslim country. Soon after the Partition was enacted (and before) Hindus, particularly those of the middle class, had started leaving East Bengal for Calcutta and beyond, and many of his friends wonder why Shashikanta does not join them. The simple answer is, 'Why should I? This is my home.' The film proceeds to flesh out this skeletal reply.

One very important feature of the film is the endeavour to establish the essence of 'home' in order to give credibility to what some see as Shashikanta's obstinacy. Children are very important to this film, appearing mainly in their play, but also in some of their trials in engaging with the adult world. Evident in all of this is a pervasive innocence, tranquillity and communal integration. The children recognise communal difference, as in the childish notion that 'black ants don't bite, red ants do, so black ants are Muslim and red ants are Hindu', but that light-hearted discrimination does not compromise their playing together on equal terms. One significant part of their play is in preparing a feast; they work as a team in assembling and cooking their ingredients and then Hindu and Muslim sit down to dine together. Of course, the elements are fake, but the director's simple point stands nevertheless.

So much of the film reveals a visual serenity. Narail by the Chitra represents a life that is relaxed and peaceful; the only threat of a disturbance to this calm is in not knowing if or when the mad beggar is going to jump out from behind a tree and demand alms. Unrest and disquiet elsewhere are heard of in conversation or in radio news bulletins; we see none of it in Narail, and despite warnings from well-wishers concerned for his safety, Shashikanta—as far as we can see—is not witness to any turmoil either. It is important to remember that most of his friends are Muslims; indeed, in a country with a rapidly dwindling Hindu population, it is worthy of note that he has friends at all, let alone so many. In this film, as in so many others, the general situation is depicted while the exceptions are by no means ignored. There are moments during *Chitra Nadir Pare* when we might tend to see the rule as the exception and the exception as the rule.

Most of those who want Shashikanta to leave are solely concerned for his safety and that of his children and their elderly aunt, but it cannot be denied that there are those with ulterior motives, the most common being an appetite for Shashikanta's property. If he should put it up for sale, he would be, like a beggar, left without choice and get considerably less than what it would fairly be worth. If he should leave it temporarily, intending to come back 'when things settle down', he would risk having it claimed by squatters or, legally, by the government as alien property, or even by refugees coming from the other direction. Shashikanta is aware of all this. He is also aware of other Hindus who are reminded by bigots throwing stones on their roofs at night that they should leave. An unmarried daughter, too, is indeed a cause for worry.

Throughout the film, Shashikanta's temperament remains consistent and unperturbed. He listens to arguments for emigration and even expresses respect for some, but he remains utterly implacable in his resolve to end his days in his own home. Shashikanta is not being stubborn but is seen as a man whose roots were set long before and who cannot agree to the extirpation of those roots by argument and logical decision. He says to the teacher, Nripen, 'Don't you realise a place has a soul? After these banks of the Chitra, Heaven itself could not be more attractive to me.' Violence does come to Narail, as evinced by the gang rape and subsequent suicide of a young widow. However, before things get any worse, Shashikanta suffers a heart attack on the steps leading down to the river and he dies a quick and peaceful death in a place which is, at least for him, equal to heaven.

Although quite some years have passed since the Partition was enacted, simmering communal friction continues. Incidents in India, often in response to some kind of provocation by

Pakistan, prompt the urge for reprisal among some elements in East Pakistan. Shashikanta had the good fortune of dying before this but the threat remains for his daughter, Minoti and her elderly aunt. They have no choice but to submit to what Shashikanta for so many years had steadfastly resisted. The film ends with the two of them on the bus headed for Calcutta.

Abar Ashibo Phire

Supriyo Sen's documentary film, *Abar Ashibo Phire* ('The Way Back Home', 2003) might question the notion of Bengaliness superseding communal identity. The structure of the film is provided by an elderly couple (Supriyo's parents), who fled East Pakistan 50 years ago for West Bengal, visiting their childhood home in what they once knew as East Bengal. While happiness is prominent in memory, much of the first half of the two-hour film details the reasons for their flight. Both the man and the woman recall what to many would be an idyllic life, but memory is particularly sharp and indelible when it comes to the nightmare that eclipsed that happiness forever. Violence was always close. Mindless thuggery stalked the streets of towns and villages, riots could break out at any time, and even egress from the country—by steamer, train or on foot—was fraught with danger. Local thugs as well as Muslims fleeing India for East Pakistan would mete out vengeance with alacrity on their Hindu counterparts headed in the opposite direction. Nevertheless, the perennially decent people were always there to give what protection they could to fugitives in peril and to help them on their way as safely as they might.

The elderly couple go to Barisal, their childhood home and the home of their forebears. The man says, 'I may not meet anyone I know, but I have a relationship with this sky, with the wind that blows and the trees. They beckon me.' Here is the reality: the sky, the wind and the trees would seem to be all that is left after 50 or so years. People grow old and die. Nothing stays the same. In what is now called Bangladesh, even rivers change their course. 'After 50 long years, I don't seem to recognise anything at all.' What might remain pristine and preserved in memory is subject to change and annihilation in reality. The sadness of this lies in the fact that the elderly couple are seeking their *janmabhumi* or birthplace, something that is more readily available to most people. The place where they have lived for the last 50 years is just that, a place. Yet 'attachment to one's soil remains forever,' says one of the grandsons of the police officer who ushered them across the border half a century ago.

It is when the elderly gentleman visits his old college, where he was taught English by the great Bengali poet, Jibanananda Das, that we see the infectiousness of the emotions that bind him being imbibed by the young contemporary students of the college. The old man and the young would seem to carry something in common through cultural ties that transcend lives of flesh and bone as well as bricks and mortar. The shots of graves and graveyards, however, remind us that the dead are there and will always be.

It is with a blend of joy and melancholy that the old lady remembers her beloved sister, who had before the Partition fallen in love with and married a Muslim, sadly cutting herself off from her own family. The old lady learns that she had died only the year before, but her daughter and grand-daughter are still there to cherish her memory. The significance of the connection by blood of a Hindu family to a Muslim one is not lost on the couple's grandson, who is travelling with them.

The grandson's voice is heard over:

> Partition did not create just a geographical divide, it created a great psychological divide between the two main religious communities in the Indian subcontinent. As inheritors of a common heritage and culture they have co-existed for hundreds of years, but for the last 50 years following Partition they have been divided into three countries and have been torn apart by ethnic clashes, communal riots and bloody war.

Now the old lady's niece talks of the troubles in Bangladesh created by the right-wing extremists and how she has their passports ready in case they have to flee to India!

Simantarekha

A somewhat less melancholy picture is painted by Tanvir Mokammel in his documentary, *Simantarekha* ('The Borderline', 2017). A greater number—and variety—of voices are heard here, and it is a seemingly happier Bangladesh than the one seen some 15 years earlier in Supriyo's film. Underlying the discussion is the question: has the borderline served any good purpose? It may have, given that Bengali Muslims would seem to be better off than they were in pre-Partition times. But then that begs another question: could that betterment have been brought about without a partition of the country? In an anything-is-possible world, the answer would be positive; it would also be meaningless given that the best evidence we would have to go on would rely heavily on vagaries such as likelihood and probability. *Simantarekha* does not set out to document the history of the Partition—the eastern Partition—but to question its contemporary significance.

The film offers much to substantiate the notion that 'Bengal' is much more than a convenient geographical reference; it is a cultural term that endows a profound sense of identity on anyone who claims to be Bengali, whether Hindu or Muslim. The simplest condition of the right to such a claim would probably be cherishing the Bengali language as one's mother tongue. Thus, the Partition in the east, also referred to as the second Partition of Bengal,[5] had an intensely personal effect on many whose Bengaliness preceded in significance their communal identity. However, the film does not ignore the many who indeed see their identity primarily in communal terms and values.

Tanvir's film, like Supriyo's, looks at the urge of some West Bengalis to visit their ancestral homes, now in Bangladesh, and there is a recollection of the original house being referred to as *home* long after a new one in India had been adopted. There is also a recognition of the emotional scars that came from the fracturing of families and the separation of friends, and we are confronted with the strange phenomenon of people experiencing not only rootlessness but the irony of being refugees in their own land. The importance of roots is summed up neatly by a woman who tells us that she makes obeisance to the eastern side of the river Ichamati every day. In reply to a Border Security Force officer's curiosity as to why she does that, she says, 'That is my birthplace. You cannot forget your birthplace.'

Many feel a strong mutual attraction drawing people on either side of the border to one another. Two festivals are brought into focus. The 10-day festival dedicated to the Goddess Durga is remarkable for its inclusivity and has long seen non-Hindus sharing in its celebrations. One man describes it as 'a festival for getting together.' We see the other festival being celebrated in Jessore, Bangladesh. We are told it is 21 February, Mother Language Day, and there is a shot of a large banner proclaiming the 'Unity Fair of the Two Bengals'. There are scenes of obvious joy in fraternity as strangers embrace each other and speak warmly together; security personnel keep an eye on everything and even take part in the cross-border cordiality. Goodwill is prevalent, but we are given stark visual reminders of the reality of the abiding barbed wire.

Towards the end of the film, two groups of young people, one in Dhaka and the other in Kolkata, discuss the same topic—the border. There is the assertion that the Two Nation Theory was bogus in that a religion or a religious community cannot be described as a nation. Indeed, for long, argues one, religion has been a tool of political cynicism. Another declares, 'It pains me when I see the same soil here as there, and with a partition in between.'

Mammo

The Partition had long been a reality when Shyam Benegal's film *Mammo* (1994) opens, yet in one household its effects are continuing to be felt as acutely as ever. The film tells a story about little people: 'little' because they have no agency in the provision of a context for their lives and are obliged to live within frameworks determined by anonymous and faceless 'big' people who enact and vigilantly maintain structures—like partitions—that fracture families and keep them asunder. Mammo was born and grew up in Bombay, but after the Partition she went, not unwillingly, with her husband to Pakistan. The man did not live for very long and soon Mammo was left a widow among uncaring, disaffected in-laws. Longing for familial support and affection, something that for most people is readily available, she goes to her sister, who lives with her grandson in Bombay. Given that the journey means crossing an international boundary, her experience of family affection must be circumscribed by the conditions of a three-month tourist visa.

The film barely mentions the Partition and the notion of 'home' is not ascribed to Bombay or somewhere in Pakistan or anywhere else; Mammo's heart is simply where her loved ones are. Nevertheless, the implications of the Partition are such that, unlike most people, Mammo and her sister and great-nephew are not permitted to live with the joys of family bonds and Mammo must return to Pakistan. However, there is hope, and it comes in the form of corruption. The bribe that Mammo pays requires a considerable sacrifice on her part, but the benefit outweighs the cost—a harmless old lady can stay in her hometown with her loving sister and nephew. Unfortunately, it does not occur to her to take into consideration the moral turpitude of officials who accept bribes; the man with whom she deals reneges on the arrangement and the harmless old lady now becomes, in the eyes of the law, an enemy alien who is arrested and forcibly deported to Pakistan. The border has been protected against a foreign infiltrator, three innocent and gentle people have become irreparably saddened and, on this occasion at least, the law has been shown to be an ass. Mammo left her home voluntarily to accompany her husband to Pakistan. When her husband died and her heart was drawn back to her original family, her 'home' tells her that she no longer belongs there and must go back to where she is legally accepted, but that is no longer her home.

Toba Tek Singh

Saadat Hasan Manto's short story, *Toba Tek Singh*, on which Ketan Mehta's 2018 film of the same name is based, is derived from the exchange, two or three years after the Partition, of prisoners and people confined to mental institutions in the two countries. Manto's story is brief and compact; without depth or intricacy it reads more like an allegory, and a very powerful allegory at that. Mehta's film too is brief by feature film standards, but it is also padded up with extra material. The film focuses on the new superintendent of the Lahore Mental Hospital, who is introduced as Saadat Hasan and is described as a budding writer; this is simply an easy device to coordinate the presentation of the narrative. However, the man is eclipsed in this relatively unimportant function by the superb performance of Pankaj Kapur as Bishan Singh, nicknamed Toba Tek Singh; the role has almost no dialogue, yet its interpretation is exceptionally moving, disturbing and thought-provoking.

Mehta's film endeavours to represent the allegorical intent of Manto's story in a context of simple realism, and to substantiate its realistic context the film relies on material extraneous to Manto's short story. This aim is not entirely fulfilled, largely because the depiction of the asylum inmates is sometimes rather ham-fisted in its apparent need to establish perceptible 'insanity'. Thus, the allegorical is often confused with the real. Endowing the inmates with various oddball personas means that the film lacks the simple clarity that is the hallmark of the short story and which enables it to foreground the bewilderment of the inmates in such a way as to shift the mask of insanity from themselves to the world from which they have been locked away.

Bishan Singh is introduced as a once wealthy landowner in the village or small town of Toba Tek Singh, who apparently lost his mind as a result of disputes over land. He has been in the asylum for 15 years and in all that time has not been known to sleep or even to sit or lie down; his only speech is a repeated 'sentence' of gibberish (*Up there the rumble, the spectacles of nonsense, the lentils of the lantern*). Of course, we can accept his background and mental illness arising from property quarrels, but the insomnia, the permanent standing and the nonsense speech are clearly to be taken as a metaphor, establishing Bishan Singh as a particular reality distinct from the general reality. His alleged sleeplessness might be seen as a metaphor for watchfulness, and a comment is passed on his constant standing, likening him to a tree that has put down roots. Indeed, Bishan Singh's roots are deep in the soil of Toba Tek Singh and he steadfastly cherishes that identity. His gibberish, we may assume, is something meaningful to himself and is a mark of his identity. All of this is credibly depicted.

In the mental hospital, word gets out that India's freedom is imminent. There is a frenzy of joy among the inmates with cries of 'Azadi zindabad!' but Bishan Singh is beset by the question: 'What is freedom?' And then 'the joy of independence was struck by the jolt of Partition.' Men, institutionalised because of their mental disorders, try to comprehend the new direction taken by the world outside. The Partition is explained by reference to an Englishman drawing a line on a map and that is authenticated by the simple fact that 'the world is mad.' One inmate reports to the Superintendent that another has lost his mind, given the latter's assertion that they are all now living in Pakistan. The Superintendent assures him that the man is right. 'Then you too are mad. We were in India until now. Without going anywhere, how can we be in Pakistan?' Here the asylum represents in microcosm the nation and its inability to digest wholesale radical change. One of the inmates observes that Sialkot was always in India, but now it is in Pakistan. 'Lahore is in Pakistan, but it might be in India tomorrow. Maybe one day India will be moved to Pakistan. Maybe one day both will be removed from the face of the earth.' One might be gently amused at the simplistic reasoning of patients in a mental hospital, but real derangement, in fact, is shown to thrive beyond the walls of the asylum as Mehta intrudes into his film a disconcerting sequence of black-and-white footage showing burning cities, street marches (the voice over says 'everyone was baying for blood'), wounded and bloodied people ('there was violence and bloodshed everywhere'), bodies lying in the street ('brutality crossed all limits'), and the constant march of refugees and hordes piling onto trains.

Bishan Singh adds to his small stock of gibberish the word 'partition' which he mutters as he goes about, preoccupied with what to him is obviously a serious concern. There is a long shot of him walking alone between two high walls—a picture that cogently emphasises his solitariness and his confinement—with the Superintendent's voice-over talking of his growing restlessness. He no longer receives visitors—people outside the asylum are too busy coping with the changes wrought by riot, dispossession and flight. All he really wants to know is the location of Toba Tek Singh, and yet he is unable to comprehend the answer: that it is where it always was, as that location is now in Pakistan.

An element in the film, extraneous to the short story, is the raped girl suffering from shock, brought to the hospital by a Christian nun. When the time comes for the exchange of patients between the two countries, there is concern that there is no way of telling whether she is Muslim or Hindu. The Superintendent directs that she be classified as 'lost'. There might be a passing suspicion that millions of others fit the same classification, but our attention is directed to Bishan Singh, the quintessentially lost soul. For years he has remained upright and awake, his mind totally preoccupied by the thought of where his roots are set. As long as he has been in the asylum, Toba Tek Singh—his home—has been with him. Now the enigma of Partition has shaken those roots and he has been cut adrift. At the border, about to be sent into India, he makes it clear that he wants only Toba Tek Singh: he does not want India without Toba Tek Singh; he does not want Toba Tek Singh with Pakistan. His heart is where he was and in what he understood before this cruel release into the unknown and unfathomable. In the no-man's-land between India and Pakistan, he cries out one last stream of invective in his own gibberish and collapses on the ground in-between the two new nations. The Superintendent's voice-over is Manto's in the story: 'There beyond the barbed wire is India, and here beyond similar barbed wire is Pakistan. In between, on the land with no name, lies Toba Tek Singh.' The film closes with a wistful song that asks, 'Who am I?'

Manto

In the same year in which Ketan Mehta made *Toba Tek Singh*, Nandita Das made an exceptionally fine film on the writer of the story, Saadat Hasan Manto. *Manto* (2018) presents a yearning for home arising out of changed circumstances rather than the trauma of dislocation, for here the dislocation is voluntarily and deliberately embarked upon. The film is set in pre-Independence Bombay and in Lahore in the years following the Partition, and tracks the sad decline of the great writer from the time of his regretful decision to swim with the Partition tide and go to Pakistan.

Manto is not so much a biography as a presentation of a writer's philosophy and set of values. The biographical material is slight yet sufficient to establish the *idea* of Manto, while much of the film's substance is derived from a number of his stories which are blended with the simple biographical narrative or actually fused into it. Manto, the writer, was an interpreter of life and for him to interpret life meaningfully, the material had to be represented candidly and comprehensively; any attempt to hide or minimise the essential ugliness of life would be seen by him to be an embrace of wilful dishonesty. And so the film opens with an episode exterior to Manto's own narrative but germane to his outlook on literature and the world. The episode starts with a little girl playing a children's game with her friends, and this melds into her mother's call for her to get ready to go out. She is a child prostitute and her clients are waiting. Dutifully she transforms her appearance and, no longer a little girl, goes to greet three middle-aged men. It is important that the ugliness of this situation be as obvious to the audience as it is to Manto. This is by no means sensationalised by the director. In fact, the salaciousness of it is very skilfully implied by the contrived assumption of playful respectability. To Manto, such abuse is common and the little girl is real; the transition from playing hopscotch with her friends to an hour or so later being drawn into cheap frivolity on a beach with beer-drinking, middle-aged men establishes her as a girl whose innocence has been taken from her along with her childhood. Yet, despite his prosecutions for obscenity, Manto was by no means a peddler in smut; puritans might have such a story suppressed, but he would have it exposed for the sake of the countless little girls whose lives are ruined by sexual commerce. Thus his stories are deliberately provocative. In Bombay, such plain-spokenness, especially through the medium of fine literature, does not appear to ruffle many feathers; in Lahore, however, it will.

Bombay is a city which accepts Manto for what he is and he is obviously at home there. Nevertheless, grafted to the city as he may be, as a Muslim and a family man he at least acknowledges the idea of Pakistan as a refuge from potential danger in India. Apparently he was offered a job in Lahore for Rs 1,000 a month and he turned it down. His wife asks him who would pay that in Bombay. His reply is telling: 'No one, but here is where I live. Live on the streets or in a mansion, this city asks no questions. But if Bombay decides to go there, I might go with it.' Although he is in every way nurtured by the city, in the light of the simmering antagonism towards Muslims the alternative starts to niggle at his mind. He overhears two Muslim workmen arguing about going to Karachi—they might be regarded as two aspects of his own mind. One says that talk about Hindu–Muslim brotherhood is a sham; at least in Pakistan Muslims will be safe. The other is sceptical about Pakistan as a haven, but vital to his thinking is Bombay's link with his past: 'Our ancestors are buried here. So will I be.' Then, while at a function, there are sounds of a sloganeering anti-Muslim demonstration outside, occasioning Manto to be smuggled out through the back door. Anyone can see that the reality is changing, especially for Muslims. Nevertheless, Manto continues to refuse to entertain the idea of going to Pakistan, not even with his wife for his sister-in-law's wedding.

Much of Manto's income came from writing for the burgeoning film industry, and now there is a growing controversy around the fact that some film studios are employing a disproportionate number of Muslims. The complaint concerns Manto too, along with the tension emanating from the growth of menacing violence. There is a little scene in which Manto and the famous actor, Ashok Kumar, are being driven through a prominent Muslim locality. Manto panics and frightened for his Hindu friend's safety offers him a Muslim prayer cap. A small crowd forces the car to stop and some of them peer inside. Their delight at seeing a screen idol is evident and they usher his car safely through the locality. To Manto, a perplexing incongruity is becoming manifest: Bombay is being itself and at the same time is becoming something that is by nature anathema to it.

The situation worsens as it widens. An uncle of Shyam, Manto's best friend, comes from Rawalpindi with a bitter tale of Muslim atrocity against Sikhs. Manto's response is characteristically humanist: 'Either everyone's life matters, or no one's.' Yet sectarian awareness and identity threaten to come between even Manto and Shyam. An embittered Shyam refers to 'those bloody Muslims'. Reminding Shyam that he too is Muslim, Manto suggests, 'If there were riots here, it's possible you'd kill me.' Shyam replies, 'Yes, it's possible.' This line denotes a major turning point in the narrative. We next see Manto writing at night, accompanied by a glass of whisky, somewhat distracted. Then, decisively, he starts packing a case. Shyam tries to dissuade him from leaving, saying as something of a last resort, 'You're not much of a Muslim anyhow.' Manto's terse reply is, 'Enough to be killed.' On the way to the docks he is reminded that after so long he still owes one Govind a rupee for a *paan*. Shyam offers to pay it for him. 'No. I want to be indebted to this city forever.' He leaves by ship for Karachi that night, farewelled by a saddened and regretful Shyam, but Manto knows that some part of him will forever remain in Bombay.

Manto will at no time even suggest that his move to Lahore was a good one. At the outset the picture is gloomy. A title card reads '1948. Lahore', and Manto is seen walking through the streets which are testimony to the aftermath of destruction and the sudden emptying of parts of the city. News spreads of the death of Gandhi, assassinated by a deranged Hindu extremist, and Manto is visibly moved by the awful information. He looks around at the evident poverty and homelessness, and there is an ugly allusion to the rape of women. It is a glum context in which to make a new start.

We soon sense that Manto is not going to make it as a writer in Pakistan as he had in Bombay. A moralistic, censorious disregard for his work and a cavalier approach of some editors in the payment of dues make him more and more outrageous, even deliberately offensive; he is also seen to be drinking more. When his house is ransacked by police seeking evidence of obscene writing, nothing is found. He is asked where it all is, and he writes down for them his old address in Bombay, telling them that everything worthwhile of his is there. It is as much a statement of personal regret and longing as it is an attempted putdown of a philistine police officer.

His story *Cold Meat* lands him and his publisher in court on obscenity charges. There is a condensed enactment of the story, allowing the audience to judge how 'obscene' it is. What hurts Manṭo most is the view of the poet and editor, Faiz Ahmad Faiz, that the story is not obscene, but it is not great literature either. Eventually, the charge is upheld; the judge finds that the story 'goes against the moral standards of this country' and he imposes a fine of Rs 300 or three months imprisonment. At one stage in the court, Manto sees walking along the cloister outside a woman he believes to be his old friend from Bombay, the eminent feminist writer Ismat Chughtai. He runs out to her and begs her to take him back to Bombay, only to see the momentarily joyous illusion turn to harsh reality. A visit to Lahore by the now highly successful Shyam only serves to intensify the pain of the nostalgia that racks the ailing writer. Falling into penury and living off the kindness of well-wishers, he declares, 'I can't take it anymore.'

He checks himself into a mental hospital as a step to rid himself of alcohol dependence and here the narrative is worked to an extraordinary conclusion. Das conflates her biographical narrative of Manto with one of his best known short stories, *Toba Tek Singh*. Having read in the newspaper of the accidental death of his dear friend Shyam, Manto is absorbed into the story of the man who simply wanted to return to his village but could not discover whether his home was in India—where it always had been—or in Pakistan. He is told it is in Pakistan but he refuses to go there; instead, he lies down in the no-man's land between the two countries. Manto's voice-over tells us:

> The man who stood on his legs for 15 years now lay on the ground. There, behind the barbed wire was India. Here, behind the barbed wire was Pakistan. In between, on a piece of land with no name, lay Toba Tek Singh ... of Pakistan and India.

This is a very similar ending to that of Ketan Mehta's film adaptation of the short story.

Manto had faced obscenity charges in Bombay, and none of them had succeeded and in Bombay no one had questioned the quality of his writing, while in Lahore it was greeted with indifference or even hostility. In Bombay he drank for pleasure, in Lahore it was with purpose. Most people displaced by the Partition had the dislocation imposed upon them; Manto made a choice and lived long enough to bitterly regret it, for in choosing to move to Pakistan he had sacrificed the respect and freedom that had defined his life in Bombay. He also lost the close and strengthening friendship of men and women of like mind; friendships in Pakistan could only be surface deep.

Towards the end of the film some ordinary men outside a teashop are listening to one of their number reading from one of Manto's *Letters to Uncle Sam*, published in a newspaper:

> I was born in a place that is now in India. My mother is buried there. My father is buried there. My first-born child, Arif, is also buried there. But that is no longer my country. Now my country is Pakistan. Like my country, I was divided for the sake of freedom. You can imagine what freedom is like for a bird with clipped wings.

Later, a title card tells us that Manto died at the age of 42.

Khancha

An unusual treatment of the heart-and-home narrative is given by the Bangladeshi filmmaker Akram Khan in his film *Khancha* ('The Cage', 2017) based on the 1967 short story of the same name by Hasan Azizul Huq. The films discussed in this chapter until now portray the heartache associated with being separated from home. *Khancha* tells the story of a family that wants to be separated from home, but finds that it cannot be; hence the meaning of the title, 'home' being a 'cage' or an agent of entrapment. One might take the view that *Khancha* is not really a Partition film at all as the change from East Bengal to East Pakistan is little more than a narrative-enabling side issue in it.

There is indeed very little focus on the division of the country and the needs of the minority community to adjust to the changes wrought, but on the other hand, the film may well be interpreted as a depiction of a dream that was at once generated and shattered by the Partition.

Khancha focuses on a particular aspect of displacement. A popular fancy of the time was the vision of convenience based on the reality that Bengali Hindus were migrating west while Muslims were migrating east. The notion of simply swapping houses was an appealing one in that it promised to save a good deal of trouble and minimise economic loss. In some cases this turned out to be so and there were people who came through the mass dislocation wounded minimally, if at all. However, the simplistic vision of convenience was not so simple, as there were indeed many factors militating against smooth settlement. There were those who kept hawk-like watch on a house and moved in literally minutes after the migrating occupants moved out, thus making it difficult if not impossible for prospective immigrant occupants to settle there. In time, the government found it profitable to involve itself in property exchange, exploiting the potential for raising taxes and profiting from sales in the case of defaults. The most common problem was the difficulty of achieving parity, as no one would willingly exchange a fine house for a poor one.

Khancha concentrates on the matter of relocation, and has very little to offer concerning its causes. The sorrow in forsaking one's home and all that goes with it is brought out early in the film when Hiran comes across Nalini at the river bank. Nalini's family and few belongings are in a boat that he is about to board as he tearfully bids farewell to his friend, Hiran. The camera dwells on the solemn faces of the family members, some of whom are sobbing quietly. Then there is an extended shot of the boat slowly drifting out of the frame.

While Hiran is visibly moved by the pathos of this little scene, it does not deter him from heading in the same direction himself, for soon we see him showing a prospective buyer around his own house and land. The house was clearly a splendid residence once, but is now in a state of dilapidation. The prospective buyer is already thinking of demolition and reconstruction, and then goes off to inspect another property. As there would seem to be competition in this particular market, there must therefore be bargaining power on the part of buyers, and Hiran soon realises that a sale or exchange will be no easy matter.

While the film does not deal much with the reasons goading people like Hiran to leave their homes and go west, Hiran's wife Sarojini sees the significant element of distress and hardship—recently experienced by Nalini and his family—in the substantial sacrifice involved in leaving one's home. This is inherent in the realisation that what one gets in return must be enough to make the sacrifice worthwhile, and herein lies the doubt that constantly clouds the intention, making it more of a dream than a determination. Quite sensibly Sarojini expresses the view that the ties of affection might more likely be loosened if they were to leave quickly, but circumstances, and perhaps her husband's lack of drive, conspire to prevent any chance of expedition. Her observation that 'everybody seems to be leaving' corroborates the perception of difficulty in negotiating a mutually satisfactory deal.

There is indirect reference to riots in some part of the country; the youngest son, Bhabla, is beaten by school bullies; and another family decides to move away, but there is nothing in any of this to strongly urge Hiran to make a decisive move. There is general economic hardship, particularly in rural areas, and Hiran's homeopathy practice suffers from his patients' inability to pay his fees. The suggestion that things would be no better elsewhere emerges from the case of the family who came from the west and are now living in the house that Nalini and his family left; the little boy is suffering from malnutrition and the little girl's marriage is being arranged, probably because they cannot afford to keep her. The difficulties being endured by Hiran's family are certainly more general than particular.

Sarojini might be quite right in her wry comment, 'They think they'll live like kings when they get here,' but she does not seem to think that the same principle would apply to them when they go 'there'. Indeed, Hiran's father begging his son for a coin so he can pay a barber for a shave—his own old hands cannot hold the razor anymore—is an indication of how financially difficult a satisfactory exchange would be for them.

India is perceived through dream, especially by Sarojini. She asks if they could go to a place like their own, with rivers and trees, 'the same birds and the same sky'. Sarojini and Pushpa talk wistfully of the school the little girl will go to, and Hiran expresses some excitement about going to such a big country with so much to see. Ten years after the Partition he comes home one day with sweets to celebrate a deal he says is almost concluded. By now Sarojini is emotionally exhausted and listless. All she wants is a small garden where she can grow flowers. Indeed, both of them would seem to have lost all hope in the future. A shot of Hiran sitting at his desk, looking through the barred window (an easy though not inappropriate symbol of the film's title), shows him notice a piece of stonework falling away from a crumbling wall. It seems, however, that he has already accepted the reality of decay.

The reality of decay is closely linked to the reality of the humdrum, and it is this essential ordinariness of life that more than anything ties them inextricably to where their roots were set years ago. The action consequent on the idea of pulling up those roots and adventurously embarking on a new life in another country is faced with constant confrontation with the routine actualities of life: financial difficulty, the dereliction of the house, bringing up children, at least one of whom is inclined to waywardness, mourning the death of a child from snakebite, and Hiran's father suffering a stroke. As the reality of the humdrum becomes more and more oppressive, escape from it becomes more and more a dream.

Both Hiran and Sarojini are tied to the past, ensuring that they are even more strongly tied to the present. Two largely symbolic elements are offered to highlight this. One is a simple family photograph which falls from its shelf. The glass shatters, symbolising the dissolution of what memories might be evoked by the picture. Here there is a flashback as Sarojini fondly recalls the day when it was taken. The family was extended then and there were people, both loved and loving, who are no longer present. There was fun and laughter, and there was innocent naughtiness from Hiran towards Sarojini. A wan smile passes over Sarojini's face as she realises, perhaps, that the past happiness is no more. The other symbolic element is music. There is a scene in which Sarojini is sitting with Pushpa in the kitchen preparing a meal, and spontaneously breaks into a song of Tagore. Her father-in-law, husband and daughter are utterly enchanted and express wonder that she has not sung for so long. Maybe it is nostalgia that urges Hiran to brush the dust off his sitar and start playing it again, evincing considerable talent as he plays. In all art there is creativity and in music especially there is the joy of self-expression. Living a life of entrapment has become inescapably joyless. Sarojini is resigned to this joylessness; Hiran escapes it by finding refuge in the sitar.

An awareness of the passing of time in *Khancha* is facilitated by five title cards indicating the years 1948, 1953, 1954, 1957 and 1964. For 17 years, the notion of relocation, while often discussed, has been so little acted upon that it is now just a yearning, a dream enmeshed in the humdrum of humble rural life. For Hiran, trapped in his cage, the dream is beyond him and has been gradually replaced in his inner yearnings by the solace he finds in music. For Sarojini, however, the dream, with little or no hope of fulfilment, still offers a kind of make-do liberation—as long as she is able to dream it. After the 1964 title card, we see her, visibly weakened by age, climbing the stairs to the roof, where Hiran is playing his sitar. Eventually he announces to her that the dream is over: 'We are not going anywhere anymore.' He mentions the very real difficulties in relocating and the conspiracy of circumstances that has impeded their efforts for so long. On balance, he concludes, it would seem that they are better off staying. 'At least we are getting something to eat, but people are starving over there.' He acknowledges that it is indeed nice to think about relocating, but to get up and actually leave is not. He chuckles, seemingly amused by it all, then loses himself in his music once again. Sarojini, however, is shattered. Her stern gaze is fixed on him, a tear rolling down her cheek. Then her sadness and disbelief turn to rage. She picks up a stick and smashes the sitar and hurls the lamp onto the floor. As she moves menacingly toward Hiran, the film ends with his pleas for her restraint.

There is a final title card, citing four apposite lines of the poet Jibanananda Das, which may be loosely translated as:

> 'It makes no difference wherever you decide to go.
> The ghosts of hunger, pain and separation will be there.
> Wherever your desires lead you, sorrow will go with you.'
> —So says the pipal tree, its head reaching high into the darkness.

Even 17 years after the event, the Partition has been substantially relevant to the destruction of a marriage and perhaps worse. It destroyed not only people and families but also their dreams.

Tahader Katha

Finally we may look at the notion of dream and home in the light of Buddhadeb Dasgupta's beautiful film, *Tahader Katha* ('Their Story', 1992). Here 'home' has a much more abstract meaning than it has in any of the other films discussed in this chapter and is, therefore, more difficult to define. Other than 'somewhere in what was East Bengal' there is no specific spatial indication such as 'Narail on the bank of the Chitra', 'Bombay', or even 'the other side of the river'. Indeed, Shibnath's Taherpur is closer perhaps to Manto's Toba Tek Singh—something intensely personal and tightly confined in the heart and soul of one man—although to Bishan Singh his home remains a reality, a burning beacon, while to Shibnath 'home' is an ideal, yet to be achieved. It has no spatial actuality nor can it be expressed in temporal terms, such as the calendar picture in Ghatak's *Nagarik* and the framed photograph in his *Meghe Dhaka Tara*. Shibnath's Taherpur is given no more substance than its mere mention, for what Shibnath longs for is an idealist's view of the future from a point in time some 11 years earlier; however, the new India that he and like-minded patriots were willing to give up their lives fighting for would still seem to be illusory.

To Dasgupta the partition of the country serves primarily to emphasise the partition between Shibnath's dreams and the socio-political reality in which, by the design of others, he finds himself. This personal or psychological partition is rooted in the fact of Shibnath's temporary suspension from history, as though he were isolated for a decade or so in some state of social paralysis, totally unaware of the momentous changes that were occurring in India and the endeavours that people were making to adapt to them. Shibnath, the extremist freedom fighter, was sentenced to life imprisonment in 1939 for killing a policeman and incarcerated in the notorious Cellular Jail in the Andaman Islands. This marks the first stage of his personal partition: cut off from Taherpur and his wife and daughter, he would not see his son, yet to be born when Shibnath was convicted, until the boy is 11 years old. After Independence he was transferred to a mental asylum for three years and then sent 'home', but home was now somewhere else. He is reunited with his wife and children, no doubt, but after an absence of 11 years, and in a strange place, he hardly knows them. Unaware of the controversy that led to the redrawing of lines on the map, nor having witnessed the horrors manifest in its enactment, the Partition seems like a fantasy to Shibnath. His erstwhile friend, Bipin Gupta, tries to explain to him that what he thinks of as his home is now in a foreign country; indeed, East Bengal has become that foreign country. Shibnath also learns that his infant daughter is now a young woman and that he has an 11-year-old son. Shibnath's wife, Hemangini, tells him of the forced dislocation of millions and the riots and destruction that went with it. She relates to him their own escape from 'home'—at midnight, during a storm in which his father and brother drowned and his mother disappeared. Shibnath's reaction to all this is enigmatic. His apparent indifference might suggest insensitivity, or reflect moral strength, or maybe he simply cannot comprehend a piece of history from which he was completely detached.

Shibnath has already endured more than his fair share of physical and emotional suffering and, possibly, he can endure even more. What he cannot abide by, however, is the moral decline that is starkly obvious to him on his return to freedom. He tells his son, 'If I had known the world would be like this, I wouldn't have brought you into it.' The new India, as Shibnath sees it, is a land for opportunists where self-advancement by any means is the dominant ideal. Prominent characters represent glaring aspects of this moral decline. Bipin Gupta is typical of those who would use their part in the freedom movement—no matter how small and fleeting—to advance themselves in the new democracy. More poetically we might see Abdullah and his dwarf symbolising the fake values of the new era, while the itinerant peddler of trinkets represents its shallow pretensions. It is Shibnath's old comrade-in-arms, Mohitosh, still carrying on the idealist's struggle, who cogently describes the failure of the new India. The foreign imperialists have gone, he observes, and now there is 'a worse raj, a caterpillar raj, crawling all over and under the throne, and for just a little gain they will eat each other's vomit.'

The Partition of India, as it impinges on the life of an idealist dreamer like Shibnath, is in fact many partitions, not one. It has denied him home, as it has millions of others; it has caused divisions in his own family and even deeper divisions between himself and the rest of the village; it has cultivated moral divisions in a world increasingly run by inferior people bereft of any worthy ideals; it has belittled and destroyed his dreams. That which his heart once called home was never truly his; that is why he and Mohitosh and so many others like them fought to make it free. They preserved their dreams for a noble future, but those dreams were dispelled by the grand overreaching Partition, and Shibnath was ultimately sent home—to prison.

'Home' means different things to different people. It could mean a profound sense of belonging, with attendant affection, security and contentment. It might offer a connection with the past through heirlooms, memorials or even a graveyard. Home is often where friends are and where meaningful relationships are forged and prosper, where a career burgeons and success is realised, where love provides fulfilment and where memories come alive. And there is, as *Shankhachil* establishes, the fact that home is so often a cultural reality, built up over a long time by many people over many generations. *Abar Ashibo Phire* and *Simantarekha* are replete with undying memories and with memories that long seemed dead being awakened on a visit, after years, to what was once home. In *Mammo*, the old lady's yearning is not so much for home as a place but as an entity that accommodates the very few remainders of family with whom she can find identity and love. Shashikanta, the lawyer living beside the river Chitra, wins in his determination not to leave his home, dying beside his beloved river, but the rest of his family are not so blessed. The end of Manto's life is marked by intense regret at leaving a city that flowed in his blood for another that poisoned it. His most famous character, Bishan Singh, impassioned yet deranged, also yearns for what he knew in another time as home, and lies down to die when he learns that home is now in another country. The marriage in a cage might have been happier had they been tormented enough to flee; however, as long as the choice remained with Hiran, his heart remained an impediment to his mind. In Ghatak's films, 'home' takes on a temporal sense, overwhelming the spatial. One of life's great tragedies is the sundering of the self from home. The heart may always stay there, but the rest of the self is obliged to migrate and journey, sometimes lifelong, in quest of an identity and some sense of belonging in alien territory among people who may never really be embraced as one's own. And maybe home is yet to be realised after the rule of a foreign power; yet if the realisation is unfulfilled, the continuing separation is every bit as painful.

These are just some of the things that the Partition did to millions of people.

Notes and References

1. The old spelling of what is now Dhaka.
2. The film was not released until September 1977, a year after Ghatak's death.
3. The title is the name of a river.
4. An area that extends on both sides of the border.
5. The first was Lord Curzon's division of the province in 1905, which was revoked in 1911.

eight

Reverberations

Jinnah's Two Nation Theory was not a convincing argument for the need to partition India; the claim that two religious communities are separate nations is, at the very least, tenuous. Yet it provided the proponents of Pakistan with a case that could be endlessly reiterated, so manufacturing 'truth' by repetition and strengthening it by the circumstantial 'evidence' of incited communal riots, for example. The essence of their claim was that given the differences between the substantial minority community and the dominant majority community, social cohesion would be an impossibility and that unrest—such as the kind Jinnah himself had stirred up with his Direct Action campaign—would be the rule. Jinnah's case was that national integration was doomed to fail as long as the substantial minority were not provided with a state of their own. However, the same solicitude was not extended to the smaller minorities.

Behind the Two Nation Theory thinking lies the assertion of an unappeasable Other. Sadly, decades after Partition, successive governments on both sides of the Radcliffe lines have achieved little by way of true nation building and enduring social cohesion, having failed to make social and cultural integration between the two communities an achievable proposition. In this chapter there is a focus on this want of social cohesion in some films that deal with three cataclysmic events arising out of the generalised perceptions of Otherness in Pakistan and India long after 1947: the Bangladesh Liberation War of 1971, the anti-Sikh riots of 1984 and the Godhra massacre of 2002.

Pakistani nationalism was, in theory, easy to cultivate and establish as the vast majority of the population shared in the one egalitarian religion. However, this did not take into account ethnic and cultural differences, and soon there developed dissension and conflict emanating largely out of that neglect. The causes of the civil war in East Pakistan can be traced to the earliest years of independence, yet the government, planted in West Pakistan and dominated by the interests of the landlords and industrialists there, seemed unable or unwilling to read the writing on the wall. This blindness was particularly characteristic of the years during which Pakistan was governed by militarists.

Children of War

There is a substantial and varied filmography dealing with the Bangladesh War, with most of the films being made by Bangladeshi filmmakers.[1] These range from short films to feature films to the epic four-and-a-half-hour documentary, *1971*, by Tanvir Mokammel. In this chapter, we will consider the film *Children of War: Nine Months to Freedom*, made by Mrityunjay Devvrat, a young non-Bengali, and released in 2014, long after the War had ended, and one of Tanvir Mokammel's films, *Nadir Nam Madhumati* ('The River Named Madhumati', 1995).

Children of War has as its major focus the abhorrent nature of the Pakistan army. There are volumes of written testimony, corroborated in literature and other films, on the barbarity of an army whose officers encouraged their men to see rape as a legitimate weapon of war. The Pakistan military is remembered not as brave fighting men but as uncivilised brutal cowards who shot unarmed civilians, including children, and raped and tortured nearly half a million women. In depicting the military as crude monsters, therefore, *Children of War* does not exaggerate these widely established facts.

There is, however, one problem of credibility, and that is the film's being made in Hindi. This is more than a matter of nicety, given that the origins of the Bangladesh War go back at least to the language protests of 21 February 1952 and the shooting of university students and teachers—who are remembered as 'language martyrs'—protesting against the Pakistan government's imposition of Urdu as the official language of the country, despite the fact that a majority of its population lived in East Bengal (officially named East Pakistan in 1956) and spoke Bengali. More compelling than demographic statistics, however, is the passion and reverential love with which Bengalis speak and write their language. To have their cinematic representatives speaking about Bengal, Bengali, Bengaliness and Bangladesh in Hindi might therefore be hard for many to accept.

Children of War depicts the excesses of the Pakistan army and its local collaborators or *razakars*, not to sensationalise but to justify the indelible contempt in which their erstwhile eastern countrymen held them, a contempt that also animated the Bengalis' liberation struggle, thus making true Pakistani nationalism even more remote. While the film offers instances of gratuitous shooting, even the 'fun' shooting of a pair of bullocks, the main focus is on the deliberate and tactical rape and torture of thousands of women.[2]

One of the central characters is the Pakistan army officer, Mallik, a man steeped in perversion and savagery who sees no value in the lives of others except perhaps Bengali women, whom he regards as factories for the creation of 'true Pakistani' children in the eastern wing of the country. He believes that if enough Pakistani soldiers raped enough Bengali women, the present inferior population would eventually improve in character. His contempt for Bengalis, whom he sees as anti-national and anti-Islamic, is undisguised. While the film has little to say about Pakistani nationalism, Mallik's assertion of Bengali 'anti-nationalism' seems to be based on the fact that the Bengalis are fighting at all. If anything, it was the government in West Pakistan that was anti-national, treating the interests of its more populous counterpart in the east with arrogant unconcern, exploiting it as a source of wealth based mainly on the production of jute, and consistently putting the interests of West Pakistan above those of East Pakistan. To the accusation of being anti-Islamic, a Bengali character in the film retorts that West Pakistan thinks that it 'owns' Islam and that its particular interpretation of the religion is categorically right. Indeed, to see Mallik as a spokesman for Islam would be an insult to Islam. The Pakistan military could hardly be described as pious Muslims, given their mandate to rape and their unrestrained killing of unarmed fellow Muslims. However, it is also true that many Bengalis regarded themselves, culturally at least, as Bengalis first and Muslims second, and this was interpreted by more zealous Muslims as being religiously unsound.

The film offers some strong feelings towards the razakars. At the army camp where Mallik is the senior officer, and a large party of women are kept as sexual captives, the ancillary staff are razakars and one among them indulges in petty corruption for sexual favours. Throughout the country, razakars were known to perform various tasks in support of the Pakistan army, usually with a remarkable degree of brutality. Mostly non-Bengalis and immigrants from Bihar and Uttar Pradesh, razakars lived socially apart from the greater Bengali community and spoke Urdu, not Bengali. They were staunch Pakistani nationalists loyal to the government in Karachi, and contemptuous of Bangladesh both as a possibility and, after the war, as an established reality. During the war they were openly treacherous but enjoyed the Pakistan army's protection, and after the war many of them prospered for a time in a volatile political environment. Eventually, the older ones died off and many of their children, mostly born in Bangladesh, grew up with different perspectives. However, in 1971 they saw it as being in their political and economic interests to fight against the Bengali nationalists and defend the precarious future of a united Pakistan.

Nadir Nam Madhumati

One of the focal characters in *Nadir Nam Madhumati* is Mataleb, who becomes chairman of the local razakar unit (quaintly known as the 'Peace Committee'), after the assassination of his predecessor, Khaleque. Mataleb is proud of his aristocratic Arabic heritage, which distinguishes him from the Bengalis, and in his mind, sets him above them. He is wealthy, largely from ill-gotten gain and from ensuring the poverty and misery of others, as he holds the title deeds of poor peasants as collateral for loans that he has given them at the crippling interest rate of 20 per cent. The Peace Committees under men of such noble extraction as Mataleb sponsored violence and thrived on corruption. As Hindus started leaving East Pakistan in large numbers, these committees kept an eye on their property and many Hindus were slaughtered for land. However, in an independent Bangladesh, the razakars' privileged excesses would be curbed and their prosperity threatened; so they fought ruthlessly to defend united Pakistan and to prevent Bangladesh from becoming a reality. The film tells of cases of indiscriminate killings by the military, murders by razakar thugs and criminal acts motivated by greed. The immensely popular and admired Hindu school teacher, Amulya, is executed beside the river, and Mataleb exploits the opportunity to take the teacher's widowed daughter into his house and his bed.

The war reaches into Mataleb's own house as his stepson, Bachchu, influenced by Amulya, joins the Mukti Bahini (Liberation Army). The war drives a wedge between father and son, who had enjoyed a happy relationship until hostilities broke out. However, Bachchu cannot abide the fact that his stepfather is a salient force in the nightmare which is apparent to all. There is file footage of dead bodies in various degrees of indignity—some mutilated, some rotting, some as food for dogs; there are corpses afloat in the river, near the banks and more being pecked at by vultures. There is also the constant march of the refugees. Stories are told of villages being burned and of men being shot with their children being forced to look on. Bachchu and his friend, Akhter, witness a group of Pakistani soldiers executing four men. A little girl screams 'Father!' and runs off, only to be stopped by a bullet. They see a deranged and naked young woman. A fisherman informs them that after her family was slaughtered and left unburied, the soldiers used her for seven days. The girl drowns herself and then Bachchu learns of Mataleb's association with the abusers. A little later Bachchu shoots his step-father. Then there is a chilling scene at sunset by the river, where a group of young men have their throats cut by razakars.

There are obvious contrasts between the boys of the Mukti Bahini and the Pakistan military. The former wear shirts or *genjis* and *lungis*, and tie *gamchhas*[3] around their heads; many of them go barefoot. The Pakistanis go booted, wearing uniforms that at least make them look like soldiers. While killing razakars is essential to the Mukti Bahini's task of driving the Pakistan army out of Bangladesh, perversions and excesses of brutality do not seem to have been part of their way of fighting a war. Their essential Bengaliness is indicated by the boys' delight in one of them being a story-teller and another playing the flute.

When Pakistan was established, it had one overriding feature—a universal commitment to Islam. It was a Muslim state created for Muslim citizens. 'Hindu' was another name for 'Indian', so in 1971, the Hindus were to be eliminated. However, to the Pakistani mind, the Bengali Muslim was an inferior son of the faith, culturally closer to the Bengali Hindu than to the Pakistani Muslim. So even before the war broke out, let alone ended with the proclamation of the republic of Bangladesh, the Two Nation Theory was wrecked on the failure of a fantasy about Muslim brotherhood that never had reason to be a respectable theory. There were more obvious examples of division and dissension, and some very obvious reasons for them, and they had little, if anything, to do with the Hindu community.

There is a shot inside the Peace Committee office where a man accused of aiding guerrillas is sitting on the floor. Around his neck is a rope, the end of which is held by the yet-to-be-murdered chairman, Khaleque. Behind Khaleque, looking down on the unfolding of yet another act of mindless brutality, is a framed photograph of Jinnah, the Father of the Nation, a nation soon to be dismembered, just 24 years after its birth, about 1,000 miles away. The irony is blatant.

In the early 1980s, demands were being made for another partition, this time by the armed Sikh separatists demanding the formation of the state of Khalistan. In 1982 the Sikh separatist leader Jarnail Singh Bhindranwale set up his headquarters with an armoury in the Golden Temple complex—or Harmandir Saheb—in Amritsar. In the ensuing two years, Bhindranwale directed activities that saw more than 400 deaths, including those of Sikhs opposed to the separatists. In June 1984 Prime Minister Indira Gandhi directed the army to clear Bhindranwale and his followers out of the Golden Temple. As a result of Operation Blue Star, Bhindranwale was killed and the militants were removed from the temple. The violent invasion of a holy place was seen as outrageous by many and alienated Sikh affection for the Congress Party and its leader (apparently Bhindranwale's use of the Golden Temple as a separatist headquarters and armoury was not seen to be similarly outrageous). On 31 October 1984, Indira Gandhi was shot by her two Sikh bodyguards, Beant Singh and Satwant Singh. The shooting took place at about 9.20 in the morning and the news was made public in the evening bulletins, some 10 hours after the shooting. Anti-Sikh riots soon broke out and there is little doubt that much of the turbulence was orchestrated by members of the Congress Party with the complicity of the police. It is estimated that some 3,000 Sikhs were killed in Delhi and the countrywide total was about 8,000, but some estimates go as high as 17,000. Just as during the blackest nights of the Partition, brutality, destruction, rape, slaughter and looting again went unchecked.

47 to 84 revisited

Rajeev Sharma's film, *47 to 84*, introduced in Chapter 5, focuses on 1947 for the first 30 minutes or so, leaving more than 100 minutes for 1984 and after. The eruption of public violence in the latter half prompts the question voiced by Sukhmani's son, Amrit: why must all Sikhs be treated as culprits in the assassination of the prime minister by her bodyguards? Yet the question, why must so many suffer for the crimes of a few, is pertinent to much of the violence perpetrated during the Partition as well as to the subsequent descents into mayhem such as those discussed in this chapter. Why does the opprobrium for the actual culprits have to be heaped onto so many more, most of whom would have been appalled at the assassination? Sukhmani quite reasonably sees the mass victimisation of Sikhs as a return to the worst of the excesses of the Partition that first sent her in flight from her home; now she wonders where they will flee to in order to escape the present violence. To be slaughtered along with thousands in one's own country by one's own countrymen is a truly disquieting thought.

Amrit is to leave Delhi for Chandigarh to start his first job as a journalist and he is asked by his editor to put his video camera to use by recording all that he can of what is going on in the capital. The drive through the city is instructive. The car is first seen entering a gloomy and deserted street with burning tyres strewn about. A body lies prone at the side of the narrow road. Three thugs are throwing a heavy tyre around the neck of an elderly Sikh man and one of them is pouring petrol over it. A toddler cries helplessly, sitting between the dead bodies of a man and a woman. A dead woman lies face down across the axle of an upturned handcart, blood streaming down her right arm, and another woman lies dead across the saddle of a motorcycle. An elderly Sikh lies beside the road, his shirt blood-stained and a pool of blood on the ground beside him, while another Sikh lies on the road, his shirt blood-soaked. The camera slowly zooms in on the face of a young man under an upturned cart. There is a close-up of a burning tyre. At this point Suleiman, Amrit's driver, asks an interesting question. He reminds us of the assassination of the Father of the Nation and asks if there were riots following that appalling crime. The interesting question is, Why not? The film does not try to answer the question, although we might consider the role of organised communal politics in 1984, which was not applicable in 1948. The fact that the earlier assassin was of the majority community might have been pertinent too. It might also be worthy of consideration that riots are not always spontaneous; like the pig slaughtered and thrown in front of the mosque in *Tamas*, they can be and, indeed, are often orchestrated.

At this point the two men come across a rally being addressed by Ratan Lal, a wealthy, prominent and corrupt politician:

> An eye for an eye! Those who have killed our leader won't be spared. We will kill all of them. We will need to make our attacks fiercer. We have all the things needed for such attacks. Destroy your enemies! Chop them! I should see dead bodies everywhere! Turn Delhi red with blood ...

Apart from the ghastly rhetoric we might note that vengeance is to be visited upon those 'who have killed our leader.' One of the assassins was killed the previous day during the arrest; two others are in custody awaiting trial; they will be found guilty and hanged five years later. Clearly, however, Ratan Lal is not talking about the actual assassins but about their community as a whole. His harangue is heavy on revenge and hatred and lacking entirely in logic. The other noteworthy thing is that 'We have all the things needed for such attacks'—in other words, there were deliberate preparations for the massacre of people of a particular community. Partition justice prevails again. Indira Gandhi was killed by two Sikhs and the streets of Delhi must run with the blood of thousands of Sikhs.

When Ratan Lal catches a glimpse of Amrit's video camera trained on him, his innate cowardice takes over. He realises the seriousness of a video-recording of an impassioned incitement to riot being produced as evidence in a court and he suddenly becomes concerned for his own welfare. The narrative direction of the film has just been reset and it will now follow the mutual tension between Ratan Lal and Amrit Singh.

There is more evidence of rioting. As Suleiman drives Amrit away from Ratan Lal's rally, a person engulfed in flames runs screaming along the street. Amrit wants to help but Suleiman insists that nothing can be done. Then a young woman runs by, crying, pursued by five lathi-wielding men. This time Amrit makes Suleiman stop the car, tells him to look after the camera and lets him drive off. Amrit takes on the would-be rapists but sustains a punch to the face and a lathi blow over the head for his trouble. Nevertheless, his life is spared, for the thugs would rather have their way with the girl than finish him off. A dead body is shown lying slumped in a gateway and another hangs over a balcony. Other bodies are seen lying on the sides of the street. As Amrit makes his way home on foot, we see prowling young men bearing lathis, a man with a bicycle towing a small cart full of corpses, and Sikhs gathered at prayer. Amrit reaches home to find his father lying dead in the courtyard of their house, beaten to death, as it transpires, by Ratan Lal's henchmen. Inside he finds his sister, lying on the stairs, close to death; their mother has been abducted by the same henchmen. Soon their lovely house will be set on fire and reduced to ashes. Of course, none of this is in the cause of justice; it is only to satisfy the bloodlust of men perverted by hatred in a crude assertion of power over the Other.

It gradually becomes clear that there is a collusion between Ratan Lal and the police, with Lal's money being effective in exploiting this corruption. Further evidence of Ratan Lal's perfidy is the story he concocts and reports in the newspapers about Amrit being an absconding arms hoarder. Much of the rest of the film develops the feud between Amrit and Ratan Lal, but Amrit also finds his mother in a relief camp and, later, his beloved Reet. He joins up with a band of Sikh outlaws seeking vengeance for the injustice, but very soon the anti-Sikh atrocities become a memory as the love story and the tale of acrimonious rivalry come into the foreground. There are more songs and the film ends with a spectacular bloodbath, much of it filmed in slow motion to maximise the entertainment value of violence. The film promises so much more than it delivers.

While *47 to 84* implies many unanswered questions concerning, for example, the Khalistan movement, Operation Blue Star, the likely orchestration of riots and police complicity, considering the alacrity with which Sikhs were attacked, it also provides a picture of an organised massacre arising out of the collective and understandably righteous outrage at a horrible crime. However, as seen so often during the excesses of the Partition, those who suffered the brutal articulation of collective outrage had not committed the horrible crime. Many may have been gratified by it, but there was no way of discerning them from the many more who were appalled by it, and yet suffered the sanctimonious rage of the majority.

Kaum De Heere

47 to 84 addresses the ugliness of social divisiveness, showing the Sikh community as victims. Ravinder Ravi's film, *Kaum De Heere* ('Gems of the Community', 2014[4]) lionises the Sikhs in its account of the same matter. While *47 to 84* is realistic, albeit sometimes disturbingly so, *Kaum De Heere* idealises Sikhism and the Sikh tradition and romanticises its heroes, some of whom many would prefer to describe as anti-heroes.

The moral map of the film is simple. It starts with the portentous rumblings in the days prior to Operation Blue Star. There is talk of tensions in Punjab, transfers of personnel and dissent. Sikh leaders have been put under house arrest. Something explosive is being anticipated. There is no reference to the havoc caused by the Khalistan movement, so that the government of Indira Gandhi may be seen as the unchallenged villain of the piece. Then Operation Blue Star is launched, and shots of its aftermath provide visual confirmation of the government's blatant aggression toward Sikhs in its attack on the holiest of Sikh shrines. There is no mention of the Golden Temple being used as an armoury and a base by extremist Sikh militants. The serious defacement of the Akal Takht at the Golden Temple is seen as reason enough to assassinate the prime minister, while those who carry out the assassination are shown as deserving of martyrdom and of being regarded as 'gems of the community'. Such a 'morality', stunted at best, completely ignores the overriding rule of law in a modern, constitutional democracy, and it exploits religion—and religious rhetoric—to justify the worst excesses of violence. The only 'good' that comes out of it is that three fanatics acquire the death which, for medieval reasons of their own, they aspire to and gladly embrace.

The conflation of militancy and religion is fundamental to the film's religious rhetoric and is established even before the pre-titles sequence. Expressions of gratitude are shown in the title cards, the first of which is to the families of the three men involved in the assassination plot, and the honorific *Shaheed* or 'martyr' is used before the name of each of them. Thus, the value or otherwise of three assassins is prescribed for the audience even before the film begins. Prior to the opening titles there is a song sequence set in the visually splendid Golden Temple, featuring the two assassins, their abettor and a host of impressively attired Sikh leaders. The film's bias is plainly proclaimed as the song celebrates 'the gems of the community' and warns of their alacrity to fight to the end against anyone who casts an evil eye on what is sacred to the Sikhs: 'When we need to confront, we go for the kill.' The sequence is presented in a beautiful religious setting, and its bellicosity is blatant.

A narrator's voice-over then takes up the theme. Over a splendid shot of the temple complex we are told that the Akal Takht is 'the heartbeat of every Sikh.' Indeed, 'to attack

Harmandir Saheb is to create a boil in the blood of the gems of our community.' He then notes that the Government of India attacked and defaced the temple—without giving the government's reasons—an action which resulted in the deaths of thousands of men, women and children. There is no mention of the innocents killed in the violence let loose following the prime minister's assassination by the 'gems of the community.' There are some lovely shots of the temple in daylight and also illuminated at night. Presumably this is to persuade the audience of the enormity of attacking something as beautiful as this, so justifying the revenge taken on the chief perpetrator of the attack. However, there is no logical connection between the attack on a sacred building and the revenge taken. The narrator then tells us that the film is about 'that incident in 1984 that gave the Sikh community injuries that are yet to heal.' In other words, rage is to be maintained.

There is a scene in which the appeal court hearing the assassins' case is told of the simple details of the crime, and there is a final plea by a lawyer arguing that in India communalism comes before nationalism. There are indeed many who regard themselves as Hindu or Muslim or Sikh first and then Indian. This kind of self-identity does not represent separate nations, as Jinnah might have believed, but it does suggest divisions that may be exploited by different vested interests. The judge does not see communalism and its primacy as justification for crime. His view is simple: the government may be changed, but by votes, not by bullets. He upholds the guilty verdict and confirms the sentence of death.

A sequence showing the assassination and its immediate aftermath tells us why there were two sentenced to death and not three. Kehar Singh did not take part in the assassination but persuasively abetted and helped to plot it, and so incurred the death penalty, and Satwant Singh was given the sentence as he was a proven assassin. Beant Singh, nephew of Kehar Singh and the senior of the murderous duo of bodyguards, was shot by the premier's other guards in a badly depicted struggle after the two were captured immediately following the killing. When the death sentences are confirmed, we see the convicted pair raise their hands and belligerently cry out, 'Blessed is he who takes the name of the Lord!' The personal quest for martyrdom and religious idealism are conflated with crime and punishment.

The film then looks back to the days after the attack on the temple complex and, in particular, the defacement of the Akal Takht (shown very effectively in a before and after sequence, again presumably with the intention of condemning the perpetrators of the attack). Inspired by passionate outrage at this horrible vandalism, Kehar Singh is obsessed with the lust for revenge and broaches the subject with his nephew, Beant Singh, one of Mrs Gandhi's security detail. Declaring that, 'I want her to be born a thousand times so that I can kill her a thousand times,' he reassures Beant that at his execution he will not have a noose around his neck, 'but a garland from the Sikh community, and you will feel that you should be hanged again and again.' It is clear that Kehar is utterly besotted with fanatical and obsessive hatred along with a romanticised vision of divine judgement. Throughout the film, up until his appearance in court, he is seen constantly agitating, cajoling, sermonising, condemning and glorifying. It is plain that his rhetoric is persuasive; it is also plain that the case against him in court is a very strong one, although it would seem unlikely that this was the filmmaker's intent.

Kehar wants to be doubly sure of the success of the plot to kill, and so Beant's younger colleague, Satwant, is drawn into Kehar's grooming. Almost immediately he shows himself to be the man for the job, declaring his blood to have been made for sacrifice. When the date, 31 October, is set for the assassination, there is a shot of the three piously at prayer. Kehar declares that 'on the day of martyrdom there should be majesty on the faces of the Sikhs.' What is most disquieting here is that all three men are shown to genuinely believe that they are planning to commit a horrible capital crime at the direction, and to the greater glory, of God.

Eventually the appeals are exhausted and the date and time of the execution is set: 6 January 1989, 8 a.m. Family members are asked to say their last goodbyes, during which Kehar tells his son that God has granted him a glorious death. A Sikh assistant jailer, Dayawan, tells Satwant's father that all of Punjab is proud of his son. Dayawan also gives Satwant a hug on his march to the gallows. On the gallows, Satwant kisses the noose before it goes around his neck. Then, once the lever has been pulled and the two men sent into oblivion, we hear a song, over close shots of the two gently swinging bodies, which exhorts its hearers to 'keep the fire alive', apparently romanticising the execution as a martyrdom.

The closing titles are run from bottom to top on the right side of the frame, while on the left we see a procession of stills giving us portraits of the three men and their families: items of clothing, a marriage card, personal belongings such as Kehar's wallet and watch, photographs of family houses, even a picture of a former roommate of Satwant. Of course, Beant has been shot and killed and the other two have been hanged, but this cavalcade of photographs of relatives, buildings and objects would seem to suggest a lingering continuance beyond the bullets and the rope that some might find provocative.

In *47 to 84*, those who articulate their moral outrage and take revenge for the assassination of the prime minister irrationally attribute culpability to the entire community to which the assassins belong. Divisiveness manifests itself readily, largely due to the visual communal labelling that makes it easy to recognise and assail the Other; wearing a turban, for example, would be life-threatening in such circumstances. In *Kaum De Heere*, Otherness is cultivated and flaunted. With the spontaneous embrace of religious rhetoric and the conflation of religious values with such a crude sentiment as revenge, those who call assassins 'gems' make themselves and the rest of their community vulnerable to the abhorrent excesses of the thugs who claimed the moral high ground in *47 to 84*.

Finally we turn to two films related to the Gujarat riots of 2002: *Parzania*, directed by Rahul Dholakia and released in 2007, and Nandita Das' *Firaaq* ('Separation', 2008). *Parzania* offers a substantial segment focussing on the riots; *Firaaq*'s main interest lies in their aftermath. For *Parzania* that aftermath continues even today.

On 27 February 2002, two carriages of a train carrying a large party of *karsevaks*[5] were set on fire at Godhra station, resulting in the deaths of 58 Hindu volunteers. Muslims were blamed, and there was a savage reaction by Hindus against Muslims. Communal violence raged throughout Gujarat for three days, continuing for a further three months in the capital, Ahmedabad; the violence continued sporadically across the state for as long as a year after the Godhra incident. The horrible reprisals perpetrated during this time hit a new low in the history of Indian barbarity, with the violence being particularly vicious and grossly perverted. Officially, over a thousand were killed, although some sources estimate the death toll to be nearly twice that. Most of the riot victims and dead were Muslims; some were Hindus. Commissions of inquiry investigated the train arson; the guilty were convicted and tried; the courts passed verdicts. The reports and judgments were, however, contested on grounds of whether the fire on the train was deliberate or accidental; and was there in fact a conspiracy to make it look like arson attributed to Muslims in order to serve political interests and thereby 'justify' the 'righteous' communal backlash that followed. The more disturbing and sinister aspect of it is that there is substantial evidence that the so-called 'spontaneous' backlash was in fact meticulously planned and sustained by political backing and police patronage. Once again, for political advantage, divisiveness and hate were created, cultivated and exploited.

Parzania

'Parzania' suggests something like an imagined realm taken from the name Parzan, the little boy who is the film's focal character. He is focal in that he is the spark that lights the happy family to which he belongs, and he is focal in his absence as his parents and others try to find him after he gets separated from his mother during the riot. The family are neither Hindu nor Muslim; they are Parsees, neutral in any communal conflict. The first part of the film is given to establish the closeness and happiness of Cyrus' family: his wife Shernaz, their son Parzan and their daughter Dilshad. Then there is a large section on the outbreak of the violence and finally the aftermath, focussing on the hearings of the National Human Rights Commission (NHRC).

The film opens with an amusing piece of schoolboy naughtiness. Parzan's teacher is giving a lesson on the Partition of India; some of the children seem uninterested and one, who we will learn is Parzan, has his head in the crook of his arm on the desk. The teacher comes to him and demands his radio; for Parzan, as for so many little boys in the subcontinent, cricket is far more important than just about anything, even a lesson on the Partition of India.

The tone has been set, not to be continued but to set up a contrast. There is a shot of Muslims celebrating with fireworks in the street, and looking down on them from an upper-storey window are two young Hindu men, identified as such by the saffron scarves around their necks. One remarks that Muslims should live in Pakistan and that 'we'll give them fireworks'. He draws a circle around three cities on a map, suggesting that something is already being planned. This is significant, for in time the suspicion will materialise that the Godhra train atrocity and the subsequent riots in so-called righteous reprisal were in fact both pre-meditated. We see a group of young men, many with saffron scarves and some with devotional marks on their foreheads, unloading drums of kerosene from a truck. We see other young men, again with saffron scarves, placing saffron flags on certain buildings; later it is learnt that this is a way of identifying Hindu-owned property, *not* to be set ablaze. Then we see Parzan and Dilshad being taken to school in an auto-rickshaw. The auto is stopped by the police accompanied by some young men wearing saffron scarves; the simple physical association of the police with saffron is significant. The police officer checks the driver's licence and one of the Hindu youths asks if there are any Muslim children on board. The protective driver tactfully says that they are all Hindu, and the police officer hurries him on: 'What are you waiting for? You want all our kids to be illiterate like the Muslims?'

Finding out who lives where was an important part of planning a riot, which will be characterised by killings, arson, looting, destruction and the consequent homelessness. Alan, an American research student, answers a knock on his door to two men with forehead paint and saffron scarves claiming to be conducting a census and wanting to know if there are any Hindus in the house. Alan is flippant with them, even a little aggressive; this will be remembered and he will suffer for it later.

It is *after* all of this has been depicted that news of the Godhra incident is broken in the media. We hear of it over the radio in an eatery. Before the report is finished, the proprietor instinctively removes his Muslim cap in an attempt to conceal his identity; he knows from experience and from lessons of post-Partition history that he is in grave danger. We then see shots of the burnt carriages of the train, bodies on the platform under sheets, and police personnel with their faces masked, presumably against the smell. On a television screen we see a morally outraged chief minister promising severe punishment and declaring that his government will not tolerate people taking the law into their own hands. By amplifying the heinousness of the crime, he is effectively fanning the flames of vengeance and ensuring that righteous Hindus will indeed take the law into their own hands.

While life in our Parsee family goes on as if they live in another universe, we do note a degree of restiveness in the streets. Contrasted with this is the tranquillity that ought to be associated with religion in shots of Parsees at prayer and a daytime call to prayer over a shot of a mosque. Back in the streets the police announce a curfew and order everyone to return to their homes, and so the riot is brought to the screen by a few warning signs and the intrusion of an ominousness of mood.

The riot section of the film is particularly well rendered, especially in regard to direction, camera work and editing. It does not observe any obvious narrative structure (but then neither does an actual riot) and elements of the action are not followed through to any meaningful consequence, possibly because this kind of mindless violence does not have any meaning. The basic elements of Partition violence are here: communal tension, demonising the Other and indulgence in so-called righteous reprisal. Perhaps Partition violence was more spontaneous, though we have noted examples of orchestrated rioting, such as the Direct Action Day killings in Calcutta and the dead pig in *Tamas*.

The depiction of the mayhem starts with a noisy mob armed with lathis, knives and sickles and flaunting saffron scarves surging towards the camera. We see frightened people being hurried indoors. The uncle of Chhotu, newspaper boy and supplier of illicit booze to the American Alan (and to the local police), is caught in an altercation and has to drop his pants to prove that he is a Hindu. The mob is seen to grow bigger as they try to break down the large gates of the *chawl* in which Cyrus and his family live, and where Shernaz is now alone with the children. Shots of the frenzied mob are intercut by shots of the terrified residents inside. There is an ominous sign when one woman turns on the tap only to discover that the water has been cut off. We see Cyrus riding home on his motorbike through a deserted street where all the shutters are down;

something is burning in the foreground. The mob has brought a ramrod and are charging at the gate to the chawl complex. Alan is driving through the streets, appalled at the sight of all the fires. A shocking shot shows a woman being held over the bonnet of a car, being doused with petrol and set alight as her attackers dance around her, laughing. A man is thrown out of a building and falls on the footpath, where he is attacked by lathi-wielding saffron goons. His wife tries to stop them and she is assaulted too. A group of policemen is sitting and watching all this, visibly amused. An overturned car and bicycle burn nearby. Chaos is seen to reign inside the chawl. The mob have entered and are indiscriminately beating people and setting fires. We see others of their ilk rampaging through the streets. Shernaz and the children are forced out of the apartment by the flames while Cyrus, who is urgently needed by his wife, is stopped at a police roadblock and forbidden to proceed any further. A car is burning at the side of the road behind him. A bloodied Muslim man holding a little girl appeals to one of the policemen, who angrily waves him away. Back at the chawl we see the mob burst into the house and run up the stairs, beating and slashing as they go. As the place is engulfed by flames people have nowhere to run. An elderly Muslim man is brutally stabbed and he dies.

We see Shernaz holding the children and suddenly being surrounded by wild, flame-throwing saffron goons, while this is intercut by shots of a terrified Cyrus riding through mayhem in the streets as the rampaging mob bash whoever comes within reach of their lathis. In the manic melee on the internal balcony Shernaz, holding Dilshad, gets separated from Parzan, who is terrified by the men wildly slashing with swords. Her only hope is to risk leaping over the balcony with Dilshad in her arms. They are unhurt by this, but Parzan does not follow them and so gets separated from them and lost. Having escaped the house, mother and daughter are seen running across a field, pursued by a group of frenzied louts. Chhotu, the newspaper boy, chances upon them, takes a saffron scarf lying on the ground and somehow manages to deter the pursuers, so saving Shernaz from gang rape and both her and her daughter from probable death.

The police try to persuade Cyrus that his home is not in danger yet they do not let him go there. While he remonstrates with them, another mob comes on the scene and some of them set fire to his motorbike, much to the amusement of the police and a couple of bystanders. Nearby a young woman is chased by a group of thugs. She stumbles and falls, and one of them beats her savagely, most probably killing her. There are unmistakeable shots of mob ecstasy, many of them brandishing *trishuls*.[6] There is a medium long shot of a mosque, billows of smoke drifting across it.

It is Chhotu who brings Cyrus to where Shernaz and Dilshad are hiding in the undergrowth. They return together to their house, which is still smouldering, some of it still in flames. Cyrus calls out to Parzan, but there is no response. It is all a horrible burnt-out mess, and the sight of it and the dead bodies strewn over the stairs has a devastating effect, particularly on the little girl. They have little choice but to go to a relief camp.

Cyrus and Shernaz get no help in their search for Parzan. The police are bullying, venal and uninterested. The local member of Parliament, his office draped in saffron proclaiming his partiality, makes hollow assurances and does nothing. Cyrus looks for his son among a tangle of dead bodies strewn over the road—men, women and children. This scene is intercut with shots of saffron activists amidst small smouldering fires, putting up posters of the chief minister seen on television earlier. This might be interpreted as a blatant attempt to propagandise and even justify what has produced, for example, the tangle of dead bodies amongst whom a man now looks for his 10-year-old little boy. An appropriate comment is made by Alan, who smashes a bottle of his precious liquor over one poster and sets fire to another. The activists beat and kick him ruthlessly.

The final section of the film represents the hearings of the NHRC. The early testimonies come at first as a shock, for they would seem to contradict most of what we have just been seeing. Then it becomes amply clear that these witnesses—who are whitewashing the police, their corruption corroborated by the smug satisfaction on the faces of the officers present—have been suborned or threatened. One officer is so emboldened as to aggressively answer back to the Commission and another asserts that there have been no cases of rape in his district. However, the bubble of official complacency bursts with an amazing endeavour at self-redemption by the seemingly worthless uncle of the brave and decent young Chhotu. He finds the courage to report what actually happened, informing the Commission that repeated appeals to the police for help would be met with the answer: 'We have no orders to help you', and with this accusation the police in the room begin to look unsettled. Chhotu's uncle then confesses his own cowardice—a brave confession given the circumstances—in revealing where Muslims lived in order to protect himself. He grows visibly distressed as he gives his testimony and tearfully admits that he is unworthy to be alive, but then he unambiguously condemns the police, declaring that they do not deserve to be alive either. There is a gentle moment as his nephew, no longer ashamed of him, lovingly escorts him from the room. The whitewashing is suspended and the truth begins to flow.

'We have no orders to help you' is repeated by witness after witness. Some claim that the police threatened to kill their families if they testified to the NHRC. A woman says her appeal made them laugh and they pushed her into the mob. A man testifies that he was told that help would come, but instead a mob came, 'And they stood there and laughed as we watched our loved ones being butchered.' We are told that the police blocked ambulances, preventing them from rendering assistance to those in need. The filth of police perversion is reported by a woman who testifies that officers did terrible things in front of her to her young daughter's private parts and they laughed. There are reports of people being burned alive. There are accusations of corruption in the criminal courts, where the prosecutor was a member of the ruling party and saffron killers were acquitted. Then Shernaz recounts everything she saw—butchering, arson, rape, even of children, severing of breasts. She points to her daughter and says that the girl will fight the trauma and demons of this nightmare for the rest of her life.

A title card tells us that the film was inspired by a true story. A boy called Azhar has been missing since 28 February 2002. His parents are still waiting for him.

Firaaq

A less confronting film than *Parzania, Firaaq* nevertheless has its disturbing elements. It admits to being 'a work of fiction' but adds appropriately that it is 'based on a thousand true stories'. The matter of authenticity is an important one in films based on true stories, for those whose sensibilities or political biases are likely to be offended by such films might easily deride cinema—and literature—as being mere fiction, the work of someone's imagination, or worse, downright lies. Nevertheless, it can be asserted with confidence that no filmmaker who wants to be respected, let alone admired, is going to be cavalier with the truth in regard to narrative substance. Concerning the communal violence in Gujarat, there is a wealth of source material from various official inquiries and individual research projects to back up representations by filmmakers as well as to attack and bring down those whose integrity is questionable. One should not be intimidated by those who would defend their position by glib allegations of calumny.

The opening scene of *Firaaq* is chilling. We see two workers laying bodies in a big, open mass grave, trying to treat those who were once people with whatever respect might be possible under such awful circumstances. A truck rolls up and stops a little way away from the grave. The tray of the truck is raised and another load of corpses is unceremoniously dumped onto the ground.

The truck goes off. There is no communication between the driver and the gravediggers. One of the workmen is distressed to find the body of a small boy on the top of the pile. He then discovers a Hindu woman in the grave and asks his partner what should be done with her, as Hindus cremate their dead rather than bury them. The partner's rage is spontaneous and he grabs a mattock as though to kill the woman again. As was evident during the Partition, hatred and blame run deep in some people.

The narrative now divides itself into four main strands, each following the plight of one or two people who survived the killings—at least for a time. These strands run generally parallel, though sometimes they impact one another or intertwine, while smaller narrative offshoots are generated from time to time.

The first strand features a Muslim autorickshaw driver, Hanif, and his wife, Muneera, who come home to find their humble home burnt down. The second strand features a Hindu businessman and shady dealer, Sanjay, and his wife Arati. Sanjay establishes himself immediately as an uncouth misogynist, as is his friend and associate, the equally shady Deven. The third strand features Khan Saheb, an ageing Muslim musician who lives some distance away from the city's hotspots and is quite detached from the reality around him. The fourth strand introduces us to Samir and Anu, a Muslim husband and Hindu wife, who plan to escape the escalating threat by relocating to Delhi.

The much harassed and seemingly helpless Arati serves a strong moral purpose in this film as a Hindu woman with a conscience who is deeply troubled by the cruelty done to so many. She in fact suffers from an oppressive sense of guilt—the guilt of others. She often thinks she hears knocking at the door, of people needing help or refuge. Of course, she could not shelter any of those knocking even if they were real, for Sanjay and Deven would probably kill them. Nevertheless, for this perceived neglect she feels guilty and punishes herself by dropping hot cooking oil on the inside of her right arm each time she perceives herself to be negligent.

Samir and Anu are going to have lunch with Ketki and Rajat, the latter being the partner of Samir in a retail store; they will see a CCTV recording of the store being looted by rioters. 'Samir' is a name used by both Hindus and Muslims and Rajat is a Hindu name, so it might seem a little irregular that their business was looted, but as Anu later points out, the government has databases on all Muslim-owned or part Muslim-owned businesses, and there is ample evidence to suggest that the government was by no means detached from the violence turning Gujarat into a nightmare.

The Samir-Anu strand entwines with the Arati strand, as a motorbike ridden by Sanjay and Deven collides with the car being driven by Anu. The fault lies with the two on the bike, but to circumvent any trouble Samir hastily offers money for repairs to the bike, and even gives out more when Sanjay complains it is not enough. What is significant here is that Samir is in the right, but as a Muslim he is in a very precarious position. Sanjay's crass comment about women drivers is accepted with practised indifference.

At Ketki and Rajat's place the television is on and features the noted TV journalist, Barkha Dutt. A woman being interviewed claims that the activists 'beat, stripped, raped, slaughtered and burnt' women. There is an intercut with Arati massaging her father-in-law's legs, watching the same programme, spellbound with horror at what she is hearing. She is grim-faced and looks appalled as the report mentions an old man being stabbed and a girl grabbed as the mob screams 'Kill them all! We don't want any Muslims in India!' The woman being interviewed goes on, 'They used swords, petrol, chemicals on us,'—here Arati is profoundly shocked—'and even used water pistols to spray petrol. They dragged people out and poured petrol on them to burn them.' Arati gets up to shut the curtains and sees—or thinks she sees—a frantic woman downstairs screaming for refuge.

There is some consideration given to Samir's position as a Muslim, with Ketki suggesting that he is a very liberal one;

Anu corrects her with the simple fact of the Muslim actuality of Samir Ahmad Shaikh. Samir reminds Rajat, 'If a Hindu fundamentalist kills someone, you don't have to hide, but if a jihadi throws a bomb anywhere in the world, we have to hang our heads in shame.' A little later, when two Hindus come to the door seeking donations for a new temple, it is the conciliatory Muslim Samir who donates, even responding to their demand for more than what he at first offers them, just as he had done with the aggressive yet guilty Sanjay. He is asked his name (for the sake of the receipt) and he gives it as Samir Desai, hiding behind Anu's family name. Later Samir challenges Rajat about victimhood. He asks him if he has ever had to change his name or even consider the wisdom of praising a Pakistani cricketer. He also refers to the persistent humiliation of having to submit to the pants-down test to ascertain communal identity.[7] In most parts of the world identity might be taken for granted, for there is nothing really significant in one's being of a certain religion or race, but in a country where Otherness has been fostered so deeply, communal tension is a reality that impacts severely on one's sense of identity. Samir has had to learn to be tactful and in his own estimation he conflates tact with cowardice, so minimising his self-esteem.

Justification of the atrocities by appeal to some law of righteous reprisal comes up even in this gathering of modern, professional people. In the course of a heated discussion, Anu refers to the fact that innocents have been raped, murdered and burnt alive. Ketki cannot accept this without an attempt at guilt displacement: 'If those people hadn't started the violence, none of this would have happened.' Her irrationality is exposed by the fact that those who became victims of the most appalling and gratuitous communal violence and those who had by whatever means 'started the violence' are certainly not the same. Not only is the argument irrational, it is also untrue if we give any credence at all to the evidence of political orchestration of the violence.

We return to Arati, who, as we have seen, is a woman of extraordinary conscience, taking on herself the pain of the guilt of the majority. We may also see her as a conduit, first to the unworthy Sanjay and Deven, then to the suffering four-year-old child, Mohsin, whom she picks up off the street and takes home because he is hungry. He tells her that he watched from his hiding place in a garbage bin as a hysterical mob burned his mother and brother. They also killed his little sister, barely three years old, his uncle and his aunt; before killing his aunt they paraded her naked. Now he is desperate to find his father, who had gone to the market before this nightmare happened, but we cannot suppress the suspicion that in all probability he too has been killed. Then Sanjay and Deven come home. Deven has, it seems, been involved in a gang rape. A woman on the television is heard saying, 'They didn't think twice before killing my two young girls, though first they dishonoured them.' Deven, the now confessed gang-rapist, observes, 'How can you dishonour someone who has no honour?' prompting Arati to ask him, 'And *you* have honour?' Sanjay is outraged and sends Arati to the bedroom where he knocks her onto the bed with a powerful blow to her face, followed by the ingenuous remark, 'I really don't enjoy violence.' All this is watched by a concealed and horrified Mohsin, who grabs his opportunity to sneak out and run away.

Sanjay and Deven are not essential to the narrative; at best they are peripheral and contextual. Nevertheless, Nandita Das gives them a significantly more-than-nominal appearance. They, especially Sanjay, demonstrate misogyny: Deven is tainted by gang rape and Sanjay is a cowardly bully who hits women. Deven is also a thief, appearing with his arms full of merchandise in the CCTV recording of the looting of Samir and Rajat's store. The simple point to be made here is that it is easy to associate these two morally inferior men with the thugs leading the riots, and such an association would be both appropriate and justified. On the other hand, Arati is a woman of rare humanity and conscience, and it is as important to be reminded that such people do exist.

We learn more about the unbearable tensions that people are being obliged to live with when Hanif and Munna, the younger of the two gravediggers we met at the beginning of the film, go to visit Lala, whose uncle has been killed. Lala relates how he was looking after his uncle when the police advised them to go to another place for their 'safety', but there they were confronted by an even bigger mob with swords and trishuls. The three young men now start to hatch a fatuous plan to wreak revenge; however, their guilelessness makes their actions almost comic. They are distracted by a sudden loud noise from outside, and Hanif and Munna go out and see two police officers tipping over their collection of large drums of water, which are essential in the event of water supplies being cut and for fighting fires—the police are seeing to it that such a necessity will not be available to the Muslims. For Lala this is the last straw and he joins the vengeance conspiracy. Unsurprisingly, their ineptness is characteristic of their endeavours, and none of them succeed. Hanif is seriously injured and possibly killed.

Samir and Anu stop at a mobile eatery on their way home. The proprietor, Lucky, is a bright and friendly young man but he is aggrieved that the riots have almost ruined his business. He knows Samir but does not know that he is a Muslim, so he candidly complains, with free recourse to cliché, that if the Muslims had not started all of this, the city would not be burning. 'Violence is in their blood. We are taught to be tolerant, they to be jihadis ... I've known many Muslims, all bloody fanatics.' Significantly, Samir decides to challenge these toxic generalisations. He confesses to being a Muslim and Lucky takes this as a joke. Then a police patrol arrives and an officer orders them to pack up as there is going to be trouble (one might wonder how he knows). He asks Anu her name and she tells him, 'Anu Desai', leading him to address Samir as 'Mr Desai'. Emboldened by his frankness with Lucky, Samir even more bravely corrects the police officer, and as they walk to their car the policeman angrily tells them to go to Pakistan. Samir is elated, for he has started to demolish a wall.

A change is also made in another character. Khan Saheb is, unusually, watching a television programme where riot victims are talking of their suffering. There is talk of broken locks and destroyed homes and the fact that most families might have only one surviving member (we might think of little Mohsin). There is mention of babies crying of hunger and the abominable mobs throwing them into the fire. Khan Saheb has been brought down to earth with a stunning jolt. He resolves that there will be no musical gathering the next day.

The film now ties up its loose ends. Hanif is probably dead, and Muneera and the baby have merged into the great sea of human suffering. Samir realises the truth behind Anu's words from the previous night, that wherever he goes he will always be Samir Arshad Shaikh, so there is no point in going anywhere. He decides bravely to stay, and Anu, understanding this, does not demur. On the same morning we see Sanjay wake up and instantly demand tea from Arati. There is a cut to the road outside and we see Arati in the backseat of an auto-rickshaw going who knows where, but anywhere else would be good enough, so her move is a heartening one. And apparently there will be a musical gathering that morning, for we see Karim spreading a sheet on the floor, and then Khan Saheb is shown singing to his devotees. It would indeed be fatuous to give such a grim film a happy ending, but just these few flickers of optimism might help hope to continue burning in the human heart.

One disturbing thought we may be left with is the countless helpless children who have been set adrift by this cynical indulgence in destruction. Mohsin is one of them. There is a cut to a shot of a pair of little legs on the back of a cart. We see Mohsin jump down. There is a shot of Muslim faces as Mohsin enters the relief camp; many wear expressions of despair, grief and anguish. Mohsin watches two boys playing with marbles.

He then realises that he is sitting beside a bearded man whose face shows an interest in him. What that interest is, like Arati's destination, we can only guess.

The devastation wrought by the Partition, buoyed by hatred, prejudice, suspicion and ignorance, was so great and so shocking that a lesson might well have been learned and a determination never to let such a thing happen again might have been nurtured. On the contrary, grudges were borne and many were made to last. Pakistan's aggression against India and its own erstwhile eastern wing ensured the flourishing of the negative emotions on which divisiveness feeds. The antagonism between East Pakistan and its other half would seem to have been immensely greater than any dissension experienced by Bangladesh with West Bengal. The awful riots of 1984 destroyed, at least for a time, the unofficial alliance between Sikhs and Hindus in the proposed post-imperial nation-building in Independent India. The Godhra riots, an attempted pogrom by extremist Hindus against Muslims, would seem to have been a re-run of the Hindu–Muslim friction articulated in the years prior to and after the Partition.

It is telling that in a nation born out of division, many things would seem to have been more important than national integration, a reversal of the doctrine articulated in *Kaum De Heere* as Indians identifying with community first and with nation second. However, superiority, privilege and power are seen to rest on difference, and the cultivation of that difference—the old process of Othering—is always advantageous to some at the expense of the many. There are those who for reasons of political gain and an exclusionist ideology cynically see virtue in preserving divisiveness, not cohesion. The violence of the Partition, of communal disputes, of inter-caste and anti-Dalit brutality, and of dissension between orthodoxy and liberalism have simmered throughout the independent decades of the subcontinent. Separatism, division and death have likewise prospered at the cost of cohesion, integration and life.

Notes and References

1. See John W. Hood, *The Bleeding Lotus: Notions of Nation in Bangladeshi Cinema* (Palimpsest, 2015).

2. The conservative estimate is 200,000. The Australian expert in this field, Dr Geoffrey Davis, asserts a more realistic figure of twice that number. The film agrees with his assertion of 400,000.

3. A *genji* is a singlet, a *lungi* is a traditional garment worn around the waist as a loincloth or skirt, and a *gamchha* is a thin cotton cloth usually used as a towel or a headcloth.

4. The Censorship Board prevented the release of the film, until its decision was set aside by the Delhi High Court in 2019.

5. Karsevaks are religious volunteers. They were returning from Ayodhya where the Babri Masjid had been destroyed 10 years earlier by Hindu fundamentalists led by the BJP and VHP.

6. A trident, a weapon associated with Shiva, the Hindu god of destruction.

7. While some Hindu men may be circumcised for medical reasons, it is reasonable to suggest that no Muslim man would be uncircumcised.